MODERN
Hooked Rugs
INSPIRATION SERIES

Linda Rae Coughlin

Schiffer Publishing Ltd

4880 Lower Valley Road Atglen, Pennsylvania 19310

DEDICATION

For Alice, who gave me my first introduction to textiles, artistic tools, and a pallet of colors.
For Jerry, who gave me all the opportunities and support to explore the world as my canvas.

Other Schiffer Books by Linda Rae Coughlin
Contemporary Hooked Rugs: Themes and Memories

Other Schiffer Books on Related Subjects
Hooked on Rugs: Outstanding Contemporary Designs, Jessie A. Turbayne
*Hooked Rugs Today: Strong Women, Flowers, Animals, Children, Christmas,
    Miniatures, and More – 2006*, Amy Oxford
*Hooked Rugs Today: Holidays, Geometrics, People, Animals, Landscapes, Accessories,
    and More – 2006*, Amy Oxford
The Big Book of Hooked Rugs: 1950-1980s, Jessie A. Turbayne
The Complete Guide to Collecting Hooked Rugs: Unrolling the Secrets, Jessie
    A. Turbayne
The Hooker's Art: Evolving Designs in Hooked Rugs, Jessie A. Turbayne
Hooked Rug Treasury, Jessie A. Turbayne
Hooked Rugs: History and the Continuing Tradition, Jessie A. Turbayne
Punch Needle Rug Hooking: Techniques and Designs, Amy Oxford

Front cover images: (clockwise from bottom left) "Mermaid" by
Patsy Becker, "Come and See the Exhibition" by Kei Kobayashi, "Brin-
diamo con Rosa" by Alice Rudell, "An American Cowboy" by Marja
Walker, "Circus Tiger" by Arne Nyne, "Eve Transformed" by Linda Tindal
Davis, "Family Portrait – Five Generations" by Gail F. Horton.
Title page images: (clockwise from top left) "Bluebirds with Nest"
by Pauline Forward, "Esther" by Patty Yoder, "Sanctuary" by Mary
Anne Wise.
Back cover images: (clockwise from bottom left) "Harriet Tub-
man" by Elizabeth Horner, "Red Hot and Blue" by Wayne Bressler,
"The First American" by Nancy L. Himmelsbach, "American Bison" by
Jon Ciemiewicz.
Author photograph by Ed Wissner.

Copyright © 2007 by Linda Rae Coughlin
Library of Congress Control Number: 2007926904

Covers and book designed by: Bruce Waters
Type set in Van Dijk/Arrus BT

ISBN: 978-0-7643-2631-8
Printed in China

Published by Schiffer Publishing Ltd.
4880 Lower Valley Road
Atglen, PA 19310
Phone: (610) 593-1777; Fax: (610) 593-2002
E-mail: Info@schifferbooks.com

For the largest selection of fine reference books on this and related subjects,
please visit our web site at www.schifferbooks.com
We are always looking for people to write books on new and related subjects. If you have an idea for a book please contact us at the above address.

This book may be purchased from the publisher.
Include $3.95 for shipping.
Please try your bookstore first.
You may write for a free catalog.

In Europe, Schiffer books are distributed by
Bushwood Books
6 Marksbury Ave.
Kew Gardens
Surrey TW9 4JF England
Phone: 44 (0) 20 8392-8585; Fax: 44 (0) 20 8392-9876
E-mail: info@bushwoodbooks.co.uk
Website: www.bushwoodbooks.co.uk
Free postage in the U.K., Europe; air mail at cost.

CONTENTS

ACKNOWLEDGMENTS

I would like to thank the following people for all their help in making this book possible. Carol Glennon, who was always there to lend a hand. Her computer skills are amazing, her friendship a gift. Roberta Smith, for all the time and effort she devoted to giving this book a thorough proofreading. Carrie Bell Jacobus for always being there. My husband, Jerry Coughlin, and Clio Hotue, for all their creative input. Donna Baker, my editor, for all her skills in making this a beautiful book.

Kind acknowledgments to all artists, curators, photographers, and others who are a part of this book and have been so helpful with getting me all that was needed to make this book possible: Jennie Adcock, Mary Raymond Alenstein, Polly Alexander, Karin L. Allen, Angela Andetta, Susan Andreson, Jean Archer, Hiroshi Ariyoshi, Gavin Ashworth, Nancy Bachand, Valentine S. Bachmann, Dwayne Bailey, Jean Baldyga, Sharon Ballard, Ellen Balser, Judy Banfield, Bette Barker, Sandra J. Barnhart, Myra Barss, Carole K. Bartolovich, Barbara Barton, Norma Batastini, Margaret Beardsley, Donna Lee Beaudoin, Arline W. Bechtoldt, Lisa Beck, Patsy Becker, Brenda Beerhorst, Tonya Benson, Barbara Bernard, Barbara Bessette, Celeste Bessette, Barbara Boll-Ingber, Janet Bosshard, Marilyn Bottjer, Betty Bouchard, Debra Boudrieau, Jeanne Bourgeois, Helena Bourque, Shirley I. Bradshaw, Wayne Bressler, June Britton, Mary Brown, Cherylyn Brubaker, Loretta Bucceri, Helen Buchanan, Priscilla Bull, Kristina Burnett, Heather Burns, Marilyn Burns, Ann Campany, Sylvia Campbell, Pamela Carter, Val Carter, Claudia Casebolt, Burma Cassidy, Celia Charlton, Madeline Cholwek, Lynne Ciacco, Jon Ciemiewicz, Cecilia Evans Clement, Molly L. Colegrove, Clark Conde, Jill Cooper, Linda Copeland, Linda Corbin, Ingrid C. Cosmen, Judith Crawford Creamer, Carolyn Creavy, Louisa Creed, Rebecca Cridler, Pat Cross, Gloria E. Crouse;

Sally D'Albora, Linda Tindal Davis, Bonnie de Blij, Davey DeGraff, Beverly Delnicki, Happy DiFranza, Steve DiFranza, Natalie DiPaolo, Suzanne Dirmaier, Judy Dodds, Peter J. Donhauser, Lory Doolittle, Dee Doria, Gisèle Léger Drapeau, Lyle Drier, Kim Dubay, Joan Dubois-Frey, Molly Dye, Doris Eaton, Erma Estwick, Nancy J. Evans, Chris Everill, Heather Falkenham, Qing Fan-Dollinger, Liz Albert Fay, Susan Feller, Gail Ferdinando, Patti Ann Finch, Deanne Fitzpatrick, Carolyn Folsom, Pauline Forward, Lynne Fowler, Kumiko Fujita, Mitsue Fukuda, Setsuko Fukuda;

Judy Gardner, Margaret Geldart, Julia M. "Scotty" Gillette, Susan Gingras, Melissa London Glickman, Line Godbout, Ellen Gonnet, Dorothy Gorham, Marian Gray, Carolyn Green, Jocelyn Guindon, Fumiyo Hachisuka, Frank Hanchett, Keiko Hara, Rae Reynolds Harrell, Diane L. Harris, Taia L. Harrison, Nola A. Heidbreder, Barbara Held, Margaret Helfand, Ruth Hennessey, Susan Higgins, Jean Himmelman, Nancy L. Himmelsbach, Diane Hodder, Sue Hommel, Elizabeth Horner, Gail F. Horton, Joshua Y. Horton, Donna K. Hrkman, Peg Irish, Renee Curci Ivanoff, Arlene Jackman, Marilyn Jackson;

Carrie Bell Jacobus, Tracy Jamar, Rita Jenkins, Donna T. Johnson, George Kahnle, Kazuko Kaneko, Joyce Kapadia, Elizabeth Kaplowitz, Nancy Karp, Kazuko Kawai, Eriko Keino, Deborah Kelley, Dayle Kelly, Diane S. Kelly, Hiromi Klyama, Utsumi Klyama, Kazuko Kobayashi, Kei Kobayashi, Joyce Krueger, Dick Labarge, Sarah Ladd, Genevieve Laloux, Gail Duclos Lapierre, Joan E. LaVine, Sue Lawler, Diane S. Learmonth, Stacy R. LeCure, Peter Lee, Thérèsa Arsenault Léger, Edie Leger-Cole, Andria Legon, Rosie Leopold, Rosemary Levin, Darlene Levy, Fran Lewis, Penny Lighthall, Maryanne Lincoln, Laurie M. Ling, Anne-Marie W. Littenberg, Sally Livingston, Edyth Locke, Mary Logue, Susan Longchamp, Barbara Ludwig, Barbara Dalrymple Lugg, Barbara Lukas, Margaret Lutz, Diane MacDonald;

Sylvia M. Macdonald, Susan Mackey, Cynthia MacMillan, Karen Maddox, Lara Magruder, Diane Marshall, Mollie "Lee" McBride, Claire McDonald, Susan McDonald, Susanne McNally, Sarah J. McNamara, Sybil Mercer, Joan and Martin Messinger, Kathy Meyer, Kathie Meyers, Michele Micarelli, Jo-Ann Millen, Joanne Miller, Polly Minick, Fritz

Mitnick, Mitsuko Mochizuki, Jan Moir, Elizabeth Morgan, Kenny Mosher, Haruyo Murata, Hiromi Murata, June Myles, Andrea Naitove, Sarah Nickerson, Barb Nonnewitz, Mary Noonan, Peggy Northrop, Arne Nyen, Nancy Oppedisano, Christian Ouellet, Danielle Ouellet;

Claudia Panizza, Mary Parker, Trinka Parker, Deanie Pass, Kathleen Patten, Joan Payton, Victor Emil Pell, Barbara Personette, Carol Morris Petillo, Diane Phillips, Judith Osler Phillips, Nancy Phillips, Laura W. Pierce, Linda Potvin, Natacha Pouech, Margot Powell, Diane Proctor, Judy Quintman, Nancy Ratliff, Denise Reithofer, Barbara Rhoads, Annie Richard, Wendy Richardson, Amanda Robar, Emily K. Robertson, Julie Robinson, Caroline Roellinghoff, Julie Rogers, Olga Rothschild, Alice Rudell;

Fran Sanagan, Janet Sandberg, Larry Sanders, Janet Santaniello, Mary Sargent, Terri Schaefer, Linda Friedman Schmidt, Robin Schwamb, Nina Seaman, Betsey Sennott, Diane R. Skalak, Susan L. Smidt, Judy Smith, Jule Marie Smith, Ruth Mills Smith, Jean E. Snow, Peggy Stanilonis, Robyn Stephenson, Susie Stephenson, Peter and Mary Stevens, Joan Stocker, Paige Osborn Stoep, Laura Strawn, Fern Strong, Amy Tenzer, Marie "Allene" Thibeault, Sharon L. Townsend, Jon Turner, Mary B. Tycz;

Britta Van Vranken, Abby Vakay, Susanne Vienneau, Rosario Villavicencio, Ilse R. Vliet, Pamela Vogt, Marja Walker, Debbie Walsh, Grace Ward, Emma Webber, Matilda K. Weeks, Mary Jean Whitelaw, Patsy Whynot, David Wile, Laurilyn Wiles, Gwen Wilkie, Janet Williams, Elisabeth Williamson, Nancy Winn, Ann Winterling, Mary Anne Wise, Ed Wissner, Edith Wolter, John Woodard, Patty Yoder, Ramsey Yoder, Patricia A. Yost, Sharon Young, Shirley H. Zandy, Roya Zarrehparver. And finally a very special thanks to all the artists who continue to create wonderful art for all of us to enjoy.

INTRODUCTION
INSPIRATIONAL SERIES

Modern Hooked Rugs showcases theme-related collections and series rugs done both by groups of artists who created rugs as part of a community project and single artists who created hooked rugs by themselves. When I first began to compile images for a book on series and theme related rugs, I was inspired by the wealth of collections that had been created. As the numerous images for the original book, *Contemporary Hooked Rugs: Themes and Memories*, began to come in, it became obvious that there were far too many to put into one book. That is how this second book was conceived.

Having a reverence for things that are handmade, I am inspired by the time all the artists dedicated to their ideas for the series or individual pieces, their color selections, hooking styles, and even finishing techniques. A recent phenomenon over the past few years, rug hooking as an art form has finally come center stage for many fiber artists and is acquiring the attention it has long deserved. Rug hooking is now enjoyed by a multitude of artists with varying degrees of skill, from the professional to the beginner.

Traditional rug hooking refers to a technique characterized by pulling strips of material through a foundation of burlap, linen, or any other open weave fabric. The strips of material are usually wool, yarn, or other fabric that will not shred when the finished rug is walked on. The simple, rhythmic technique of pulling loops has also moved to new arenas, where it has expanded to include methods such as, punch, fine needle punch, proddy, and even stitching to the foundation. Many pieces also include an array of different types of embellishments that are applied to the finished piece. Through their evolution, hooked rugs have gone from being utilitarian items for the floor to an art form that is displayed on any surface. Many hooking techniques are being applied in different and creative ways as this art form grows in new directions.

Modern Hooked Rugs: Inspirational Series features the work of 292 artists from around the world. These artists share their passion as some have incorporated highly personal forms and signs into many of their rugs. Others have done studies of the human body, locations, families, animals, nature, and even social issues. Unlike painting, which is two-dimensional, creating art with fiber leads to a different conceptual approach. Various materials featuring a multitude of colors and textures take on new character after they are hooked and gain three-dimensional quality. Some of the pieces shown in this book are created with non-traditional hooking techniques and are not typically items for the floor. Many of the items are used as wall hangings, masks, door toppers, signs, chair pads, trivets, and even pillows. Along with the rugs in this book, I have also included some "sidebars" that are meant to inspire you on your own creative journey.

It is my fervent wish for you to enjoy these diverse collections, theme-related series rugs, and individual rugs, as they pay homage to an art form that has been handed down from one generation to the next.

The artists highlighted in this book have been very generous in sharing their "gifts" (rugs) with all of us. I believe that art is not for just for one person alone but should be shared with others. That is why I am so grateful to all the artists who generously contributed and were willing to share what is personal and meaningful to them to make this book possible.

"If you ever want to know who I am, just look, I am my 'Art' and what I create with my hands."

—Linda Rae Coughlin

Please note that sizes of the rugs have been rounded to the nearest inch, with the height of the rug preceding width, unless otherwise noted. Collections in this book are not necessarily complete.

Chapter One
AMERICAN ICONS

This chapter shows the diverse pictorial representations
of what American icons mean to the artists who explored
this subject in their work.

AMERICAN FOLK ART MUSEUM
ICON WINNERS

An "Icons of America" contest, sponsored by the American Folk Art Museum, New York City, New York, had over sixty-four entries from around the world. This exciting contest was conceived by Lee Kogan, Director, Folk Art Institute, and Marilyn Bottjer, textile instructor at the museum, for their annual "Rug Day" exhibit in 2006. The museum hoped that rugs created for this contest would convey the feeling of an "American Icon." The only contest requirements were that the rugs could be no larger than 18" x 26" in any direction and hooked in whatever style the artist chose.

Featured here are fourteen of the fifteen winners from this contest. Along with the fifteen winning rugs, the judges also wanted to recognize the rug of Fumiyo Hachisuka of Tokyo, Japan, "The Rising Sun

and the Mayflower in Plymouth," which was not one of the winners because it was slightly larger than the size requirements stated in the contest rules. All sixteen rugs where exhibited at the Green Mountain Rug Show at the Shelburne Museum in April 2006.

Jurors for this exhibit were Stacy Hollander, Senior Curator and Director of Exhibitions, American Folk Art Museum; Brooke Davis Anderson, Director and Curator of The Contemporary Center and the Henry Darger Study Center, American Folk Art Museum; Kristina Johnson, Esq., rug collector; and Thomas K. Woodard, Woodard & Greenstein American Antiques.

An icon rug not featured is "Once There Were Many" by Pam Bartlett. *Photography by Gavin Ashworth, courtesy of The American Folk Art Museum.*

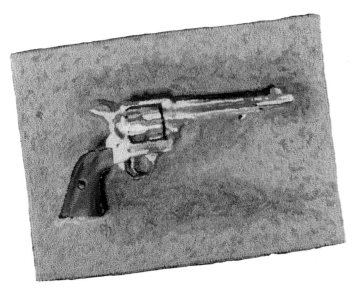

Colt .45. 18" x 26". By Susan Higgins, Eureka, California. 2005. "The ultimate icon, the Colt .45! Once, it represented power, prowess, and domination, the conquering of the West, the paradox of good vs. bad. Brilliantly conceived, expertly crafted, projectile delivery system capable of grave damage. It seemed to say it all." The icon contest "First Place" rug.

Harriet Tubman. 26"x18" By Elizabeth Hornor, Tucson, Arizona. 2005. "Harriet Tubman was a conductor on the Underground Railroad. She aided more than 300 people to freedom and her continued roles and accomplishments for humanity and our nation is undeniably incredible. I hope that showing this portrait of her will inspire people to find out more about her life and dedication to our country. Harriet's (last) dying words (on earth) were 'I go to prepare a place for you' (March 11, 1913), which sounds beautiful and saintly to me. "This rug was the icon contest "Second Place" rug.

Red Hot and Blue. 24" x 17". By Wayne Bressler, New York City, New York. 2005. "As a graphic designer, illustrator, and cartoonist, I was inspired by the fact that I enjoy drawing fast food. With this in mind, what better American icon than the hot dog? The hardest part in creating this punched piece was making the yarn look like relish."

Andy. 20" x 16". By Molly L. Colegrove, Canandaigua, New York. 2005. "Andy was inspired by the influence Andy Warhol has on pop culture today."

Model T Ford. 18" x 26". By Happy DiFranza, North Reading, Massachusetts. 2005. "The vast array of products available to the average consumer is something very American. Henry Ford's assembly-line manufacturing of the Model T car illustrates this idea perfectly. His business acumen made this wonderful mode of transportation available to the average consumer, so I chose this as my icon. I placed it on a weather vane, since they often symbolized the development of industry and are works of art in themselves."

We the People. 18" x 26". By Liz Albert Fay, Sandy Hook, Connecticut. 2005. "Working with the concept that a country is shaped by its people, I gathered images of Americans who are, or were, leaders in their fields. Choosing only Americans who could be visually recognized by most people, I included leaders in the fields of art, human rights, politics, science, history, and athletics. As the project developed, cartoon characters and symbols representing the United States, such as Uncle Sam, were added. Superman was placed in a central location indicating our 'superpower' status in the world. The border suggests another of our great symbols, our flag, which does not completely enclose the central images, but loosely holds them together, indicating our freedom." PEANUTS © United Feature Syndicate, Inc.

One Hip Chick. 16" x 27". By Rae Reynolds Harrell, Hinesburg, Vermont. 2005. "I chose Miss Liberty because I respect her and she most represents our country. She is big and beautiful, inspiring and strong. My image is pouty lipped with soulful eyes and a face that looks a little battered. Her beauty shines through in spite of mishaps."

The First American. 18" x 26". By Nancy L. Himmelsbach, Hampton Bays, New York. 2005. "This piece emerged from an appreciation of Native Americans and the kindness they showed towards others who were different from themselves. The Manhattan skyline symbolizes the transformation of nature into a great American city where people of all walks of life live among each other."

Newton 2005. 18" x 26". By Diane S. Learmonth, Anacortes, Washington. 2005. "The Maytag Corporation has been in existence since the late 1800s in Newton, Iowa. The Whirlpool Corporation put in an offer to purchase Maytag in 2005 and succeeded in 2006. This rug represents the face of Newton contemplating the Whirlpool takeover."

Fender Strat. 26" x 18". By Cynthia MacMillan, Newtown, Pennsylvania. 2005. "A true icon." Fender®, Stratocaster®, Strat®, and the distinctive headstock and body designs of those guitars are trademarks of the Fender Musical Instruments Corporation and used herein with express written permission. All rights reserved.

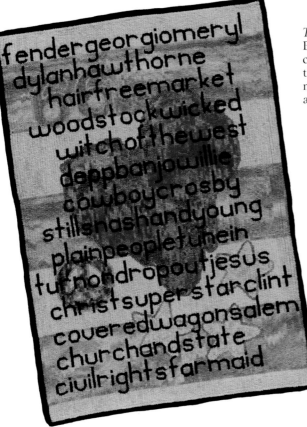

The Heart of America. 26" x 18". By Denise Reithofer, Burlington, Ontario, Canada. 2005. "This piece was created using symbols such as the stars, the heart, the peace symbol, and Route 66 along with many meaningful words that depict America on a white and blue flag backdrop."

Apple Pie and Motherhood. 18" x 26". By Rosario Villavicencio, Mamaroneck, New York. 2005. A bird's-eye view into a family's kitchen, with a warm homemade apple pie sitting on the table.

Watch Your Back. 18" x 26". By Paige Osborn Stoep, Lyons, New York. 2005. "A cowboy and his horse as they watch each other's backs, supported by the American flag."

Road Trip. 18" x 26". By Janet Williams, Skillman, New Jersey. 2005. "What is more American than an infatuation with cars and taking a road trip? Our family has a history of taking car trips throughout America. When my dad and uncle were 86 and 89 years old, they took a 2,000 mile road trip to break in my dad's new car, a Toyota hybrid Prius. My husband and I have visited all the states by car that are shown in the rug except Alaska, which is on our list and was visited by my Dad and son in an epic car trip."

The Rising Sun in Plymouth. 19" x 27". By Fumiyo Hachisuka, Tokyo, Japan. 2005. "Visiting Plymouth, Massachusetts in 2000, I saw the *Mayflower* ship and imagined the pilgrims' long voyage and their living in a new land. These people are the origin of today's America, the biggest country in the world for everything. I feel that immigration from Europe was the start of today's prosperous America."

OTHER AMERICAN ICON RUGS

Shown here are some additional American Icon rugs. Most, but not all, were entered in the "Icons of America" contest sponsored by the American Folk Art Museum in New York City, New York.

Welcome to America. 21" x 12". By Mary Raymond Alenstein, Briarcliff Manor, New York. 2005. "Early immigration to America was possible via the *Mayflower* to Plymouth, Massachusetts, and later to New York via steamship. My family arrived in Plymouth and my husband's in New York harbor early in the twentieth century, so this rug feels quite personal." *Courtesy of Mary Raymond Alenstein.*

Cowboy Rug. 26" x 18". By Brenda Beerhorst, Brooklyn, New York. 2005. A national icon. *Courtesy of Brenda Beerhorst.*

The Big Apple. 18" x 26". By Marilyn Bottjer, Eastchester, New York. 2005. New York City. *Courtesy of Marilyn Bottjer.*

Bison, Bison. 26" x 17". By Cherylyn Brubaker, Brunswick, Maine. 2005. Bison in field, mountains in distance, "flag" sky. Semifinalist in the contest. *Courtesy of Cherylyn Brubaker.*

Rosy Peace. 26" x 18". By Claudia Casebolt, Lawrenceville, New Jersey. 2005. "Using the roses from the rug on the cover of *American Hooked and Sewn Rugs* by Joel and Kate Kopp as the border, this rug depicts a peace symbol, which could be an American icon if you were looking through rose-colored glasses." *Courtesy of Claudia Casebolt.*

American Bison. 22" x 18". By Jon Ciemiewicz, Hudson, New Hampshire. 2005. An American bison. *Courtesy of Jon Ciemiewicz.*

Animal Spirit Dream Trance. 22" x 18". By Jon Ciemiewicz, Hudson, New Hampshire. 2005. "A native American who has taken drugs and gone into a dream trance to envision his spirit animal, which in this case is a bison." *Courtesy of Jon Ciemiewicz.*

Thelma. 26" x 18". By Linda Rae Coughlin, Warren, New Jersey. 2005. "'Thelma' was inspired by the American classic movie *Thelma and Louise.* In the spirit of 'Bonnie and Clyde', these two victimized women were transformed from a waitress and housewife into American legends and icons of American feminism. The words around the outside of the piece, along with the gun in the woman's hand, are symbolic of the underlying theme of female liberation and personal expression." Semifinalist in the Icon contest. *Photography by Linda Rae Coughlin.*

Iconic Liberty. 18" x 30". By Susan Feller, Augusta, West Virginia. 2006. "This design is monochromatic and is silver like our coinage. The 'Walking Liberty' image is a powerful active female. Using words and three dimensional textile techniques, the aim was to capture a starting point for women's rights." *Courtesy of Susan Feller.*

Reaching Out. 24" x 17". By Lynne Fowler, Westover, Maryland. 2005. Oprah in her anniversary dress with her hands reaching out to all the people she helps. *Courtesy of Lynne Fowler.*

On Giant's Shoulders. 18" x 25". By Carolyn Green, Essex, England. 2005. "An astronaut drifts in space tethered by his umbilical cord to the Wright's Flyer by the light of the moon." *Courtesy of Carolyn Green.*

Local Hero. 26" x 18". By Jocelyn Guindon, Montreal, Quebec, Canada. 2005. A 1930s Art Deco stained glass-looking detail of a local firehouse. *Courtesy of Jocelyn Guindon.*

Oh George. 10" x 24". By Nola A. Heidbreder, St. Louis, Missouri. 2005. "I thought the dollar bill was a very recognizable American icon. The hatchet and cherries were added for humor." *Courtesy of Nola Heidbreder.*

Lady Liberty. 13" x 12". By Carrie Bell Jacobus, Oradell, New Jersey. 2005. The Statue of Liberty overlooking the harbor. *Photography by Linda Rae Coughlin.*

Frank Lynam's Cabin. 18" x 23". By Tracy Jamar, New York City, New York. 2005. "Log cabin built by my grandfather in 1898 in northern Wisconsin. The family still uses it." *Courtesy of Tracy Jamar.*

From Sea To Shining Sea. 15" x 21". By Diane S. Kelly, Dorset, Vermont. 2005. "This rug is a result of a doodle and the American flag that flies in our yard. The doodle became waves, became one bald eagle, became the stripes of the flag with a single star uniting us all." *Courtesy of Diane S. Kelly.*

Little Spirit Cedar Tree. 25" x 17". By Joan E. LaVine, St. Paul, Minnesota. 2005. "Little Spirit Cedar Tree is more than three hundred years old. It grows on the rocky bluffs of Lake Superior in Grand Portage, Minnesota and is sacred to the Ojibwe Indians who place tobacco at its roots to insure a safe journey on the lake." *Courtesy of Joan E. LaVine.*

Free Martha. 18" x 26". By Sue Lawler, Dorset, Vermont. 2005. "Started in 2004, using images and palette à la façon de Martha Stewart in what I hoped was a fun and celebratory mode. Then I lost my background wool. By the time I finished, Martha had freed herself. Hooray!" *Photography by Erma Estwick.*

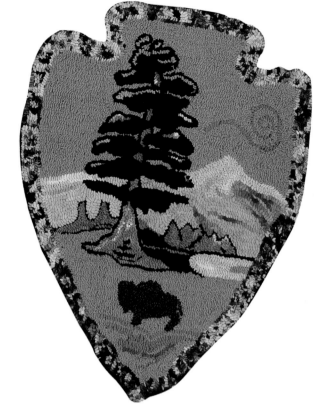

Save Our National Parks. 23" x 17". By Rosemary Levin, Corea, Maine. 2005. "The icon of the National Park, as a patch worn by the Park Rangers, a sign to guide visitors in the park." *Courtesy of Rosemary Levin.*

Purple Mountains' Majesty. 21" x 20". By Anne-Marie W. Littenberg, Burlington, Vermont. 2005. The purple mountains of America. A semifinalist in the Icon contest. *Courtesy of Anne-Marie Littenberg.*

Tic Tac Dough. 13" x 13". By Lara Magruder, Hayward, California. 2005. Icon symbols hooked and stitched with synthetic yarns, wool, and U.S. currency, create this game board. *Courtesy of Lara Magruder.*

In Spending We Trust. 23" x 18". By June Myles, Redding, Connecticut. 2005. George Washington on the dollar bill. "The dollar bill seems to be historically, politically, and economically important globally and nationally." *Photography by Linda Rae Coughlin.*

Hollywood. 24" x 18". By Mary Parker, Yorktown Heights, New York. 2005. "This American icon includes Hollywood, the Hollywood sign, Hollywood movie stars, Andy Warhol, and indirectly Marilyn Monroe because I used Warhol's 'Marilyn' colors." *Courtesy of Mary Parker.*

Hmm I Wonder. 18" x 26". By Deanie Pass, St. Paul, Minnesota. 2005. "Continuing my series of me as a stand-in for historical women figures. This time as Wonder Woman." *Photography by Peter Lee.*

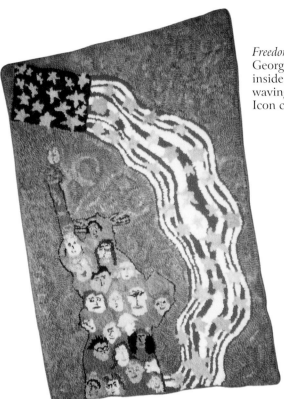

Freedom For All. 26" x 18". By Joan Payton, Atlanta, Georgia. 2005. "Many faces of all nationalities inside the outline of the Statue of Liberty plus a waving flag with fifty stars." A semifinalist in the Icon contest. *Courtesy of Joan Payton.*

New England Memories. 26" x 18". By Carol Morris Petillo, Vinalhaven, Maine. 2005. A sculpted rug picturing an old abandoned New England quarryman's cottage. *Courtesy of Carol Morris Petillo.*

Failure is Impossible - Susan B. Anthony. 26" x 18". By Diane Phillips, Fairport, New York. 2005. "'Failure is Impossible' is a quote from Susan B. Anthony in her last speech to congress before her death. She worked her entire life for women's suffrage." *Photography by Clark Conde.*

Lance. 23" x 17". By Laura W. Pierce, Petaluma, California. 2005. "Lance Armstrong racing hard in his yellow jersey. An eagle flies overhead and a mountain looms in the background." *Courtesy of Laura W. Pierce.*

Smokey the Bear. 18" x 26". By Julie Robinson, Loudon, New Hampshire. 2005. "After sixty years, Smokey the Bear is still reminding us all to be careful with fire." *Courtesy of Julie Robinson.*

F150. 19" x 26". By Olga Rothschild, Duxbury, Massachusetts. 2005. "Drawing of an older model F150 truck against a geometric background." *Courtesy of Olga Rothschild.*

Face Value. 18" x 26". By Linda Friedman Schmidt, Franklin Lakes, New Jersey. 2005. "For me, the faces of the people are what is most important in life. This piece is about monetary worth vs. self worth, monetary worth vs. human worth, monetary worth vs. artistic value, monetary value vs. the ego, and national identity vs. personal identity." *Courtesy of Linda Friedman Schmidt.*

Johnny Cash #1. 26" x 18". By Betsey Sennott, Belmont, Maryland. 2005. A fan of Johnny Cash since she was a child, Betsey created this piece for his song "I Walk the Line." *Courtesy of Betsey Sennott.*

Live Strong. 18" x 26". By Robyn Stephenson, Cummings, Georgia. 2005. Lance Armstrong riding his bike in front of the American flag. *Courtesy of Robyn Stephenson.*

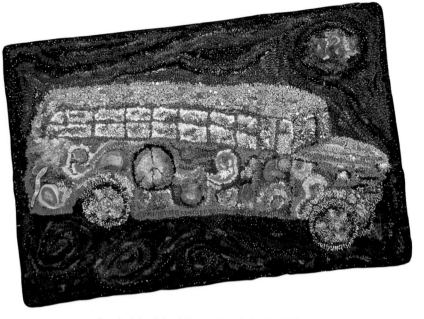

Psychedelic School Bus. 18" x 26". By Abby Vakay, West Hampton, New York. 2005. Magic bus. *Courtesy of Abby Vakay.*

Flamingo. 25" x 18". By Sharon L. Townsend, Altoona, Iowa. 2005. "From sea to shining sea and across the fruited plains, American flamingos are seen as fundraisers, business symbols, and in collections. From Marshalltown, Iowa to Marathon, Florida and points east, west, north, and south they give delight and chuckles to our hearts." *Courtesy of Sharon L. Townsend.*

An American Cowboy. 26" x 18". By Marja Walker, Tucson, Arizona. 2005. "Growing up in the west this is the only icon that came to mind." Semifinalist in the Icon contest. *Photography by Britta Van Vranken.*

Sacagawea and Pompey. 16" x 15". By Ann Winterling, Concord, New Hampshire. 2005. "Portrait of a Shoshoni Indian guide who joined Lewis and Clark and the Corps of Discovery in 1804 as their interpreter. She carried her baby boy Pompey on her back." Semifinalist in the Icon contest. *Courtesy of Ann Winterling.*

Chapter Two
ANIMALS

When it comes to inspiration, artists always seem to find a wealth of willing subjects for rug designs in their four-legged friends, the animals.

ANIMAL RUGS
BY WINE COUNTRY RUG HOOKERS

This animal collection was done by the Wine Country Rug Hookers of Northern California.

Dorset Sound Animal Tangle. 24" x 30". By Emma Webber, Petaluma, California. 1975. Hand-cut wool strips and yarn. *Courtesy of Emma Webber.*

Red and White Animal Tangle. 36" x 24". By Emma Webber, Petaluma, California. 1980. All the animals touch in the "ladder." Hand-cut strips, wool strips, and yarn. *Courtesy of Emma Webber.*

Watson. 24" x 36". By Margaret Beardsley, Frederick, Maryland. 2004. "A beloved cat that belonged to a friend, much loved and now deceased." *Courtesy of Margaret Beardsley.*

Buster Brown. 23" x 22". By Laura W. Pierce, Petaluma, California. 1997. This piece hangs as a diamond and is Laura's second rug. It depicts Buster, her long haired dachshund, flying happily over Sonoma County. *Courtesy of Laura Pierce.*

Flying Dachshunds. 14" x 15". By Laura W. Pierce, Petaluma, California. 2000. Tea cozy, front side. Won "Best of Show" at the Sonoma County Fair. *Courtesy of Laura Pierce.*

Flying Dachshunds. 14" x 15". By Laura W. Pierce, Petaluma, California. 2000. Tea cozy, back side. "This side shows Buster's deceased mother, Frisky, with angel wings and halo." *Courtesy of Laura Pierce.*

Flying Dachshunds of the North Coast. 15" x 15".
By Laura W. Pierce, Petaluma, California. 2002.
This is the third rug in the "Wiener Dog" series.
Courtesy of Laura Pierce.

Thomas. 18" x 5". By Laura W. Pierce, Petaluma,
California. 2003. "A lifelike 'cat' doll of the late
family cat, Thomas. His eyes really fool people and
they think he is real." *Courtesy of Laura Pierce.*

Joy Ride. 30" x 37". By Peggy Northrop, Sebastopol,
California. 2003. "This fantasy rug is my favorite and
my biggest challenge. Second place Readers' Choice in
Rug Hooking Magazine's contest 'A Celebration of Hand-
Hooked Rugs XIV.'" *Courtesy of Peggy Northrop.*

Shearing. 27" x 32". By Peggy Northrop, Sebastopol, California. 2002. "This piece depicts the shearing process. Notice the kitty doing all the work and the kitty hiding in the hill." *Courtesy of Peggy Northrop.*

Cody. 18" x 18". By Peggy Northrop, Sebastopol, California. 2001. "This piece was my first attempt with a 3 cut. Square pillow." *Courtesy of Peggy Northrop.*

Horse from Lascaux Cave. 21" x 27". By Judy Smith, Sebastopol, California. 2005. Adaptation of a cave drawing, hooked with hand-cut strips. *Courtesy of Judy Smith.*

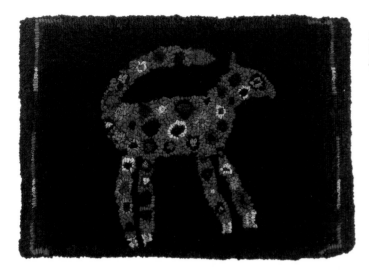

Spot the Dog. 15" x 21". By Judy Smith, Sebastopol, California. 2004. Hand-cut 1/4" wide strips. *Courtesy of Judy Smith.*

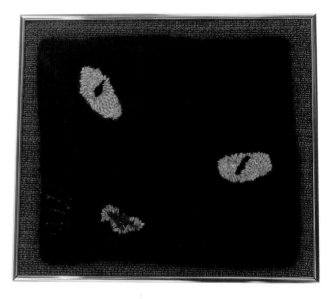

Black Cat Face. 10" x 12". By Judy Smith, Sebastopol, California. 2004. Hand-cut 1/4" wide strips. *Courtesy of Judy Smith.*

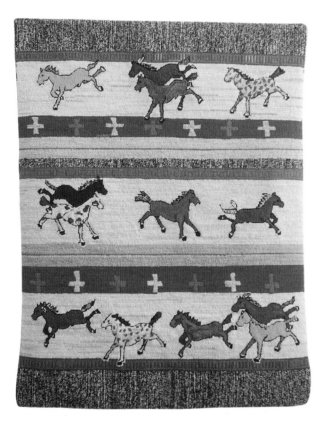

Lakota Ponies. 39" x 30". By Nancy Winn, Sebastopol, California. 2005. "Inspired by Native American drawings from the late 1800s. 'Best of Show' at the Sonoma County Fair 2005." *Courtesy of Nancy Winn.*

Sisters. 16" x 22". By Nancy Winn, Sebastopol, California. 2004. "These are two feral cats I found at four weeks old. I hooked them, then one disappeared. I am very grateful for the hooked memory. This piece took a blue ribbon in the Sonoma County Fair 2004." *Courtesy of Nancy Winn.*

PRIMITIVE ANIMAL RUGS
BY SUSIE STEPHENSON

Self-taught fiber artist Susie Stephenson of Edge-comb, Maine has created this delightful collection of animal rugs. Many of the rugs in this collection were inspired by the art of her children. *Photography courtesy of Susie Stephenson.*

Susie Cat. 14" x 13". By Susie Stephenson, Edgecomb, Maine. 2001. "This piece was created to play around with the border."

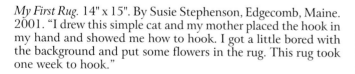

The Kittens. 14" x 20". By Susie Stephenson, Edgecomb, Maine. 2001. "My son Nathaniel drew this rug on a tiny piece of linen and it was so cute I hooked it immediately. I love the way he put the roots on the flower. His initials and name are in the background, which once was a beautiful wool blanket."

My First Rug. 14" x 15". By Susie Stephenson, Edgecomb, Maine. 2001. "I drew this simple cat and my mother placed the hook in my hand and showed me how to hook. I got a little bored with the background and put some flowers in the rug. This rug took one week to hook."

> *Develop your own style and visual vocabulary,*
> *which you can then apply to your current work.*

Max. 18" x 29". By Susie Stephenson, Edgecomb, Maine. 2001. "Max is our cat. He was one of four tigers, distinguishable only by a white stripe on his nose. The background was two old shirts (as is). I changed the border from my original plan and really liked the wiggly lines. The red dots pull it all together. Max died in the spring of 2005 very unexpectedly. My daughter has claimed this rug as hers. I love having this rug to help remember our special cat!"

Nat's Cat. 19" x 25". By Susie Stephenson, Edgecomb, Maine. 2001. "My son Nathaniel Blackford drew this picture at school for a sign 'Lost Cat,' as the school cat had disappeared. He then brought home the drawing for me to hook as a rug."

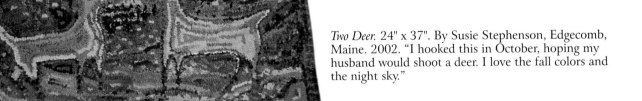

Two Deer. 24" x 37". By Susie Stephenson, Edgecomb, Maine. 2002. "I hooked this in October, hoping my husband would shoot a deer. I love the fall colors and the night sky."

Bill. 18" x 24". By Susie Stephenson, Edgecomb, Maine. 2001. "My son Nathaniel was seven when he drew this cat on a box lid. After hooking it, I tried to make it bigger by putting a braided edge around it. The background in the rug is an old plaid shirt. This rug makes me smile just like the cat."

The Fox. 33" x 26". By Susie Stephenson, Edgecomb, Maine. 2003. "This rug is of the fox who regularly comes to the chicken house for a snack."

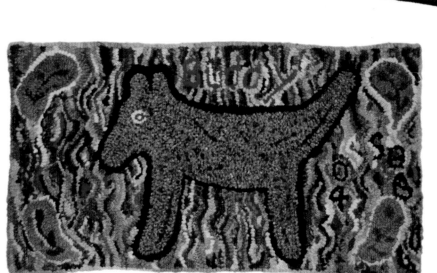

Buddy. 18" x 34". By Susie Stephenson, Edgecom Maine. 2004. "Buddy is a flat- topped antique cookie cutter (enlarged a lot). The leaf things in corners are also cookie cutters (actual size). The background is a hodgepodge of leftover wool, no even married. I think this rug needs to be used a the front door for awhile to antique it some."

Single Deer. 15" x 15". By Susie Stephenson, Edgecomb, Maine. 2002. "I love the simplicity of this deer and the gray background. I think the gray makes it look like a rock, so I guess you could say the deer is a petroglyph."

Othello. 28" x 26". By Susie Stephenson, Edgecomb, Maine. 2003. "This rooster was inspired by an old weather vane and a rooster we once had, called Othello. I love the simple lines. I made the braid around the edge to enlarge the rug."

Sam. 55" x 38". By Susie Stephenson, Edgecomb, Maine. 2003. "Our dog Sam is half border collie and half Australian shepherd. I had so many cat rugs I decided to make one of Sam. This rug hooked up very fast, even with its being so large."

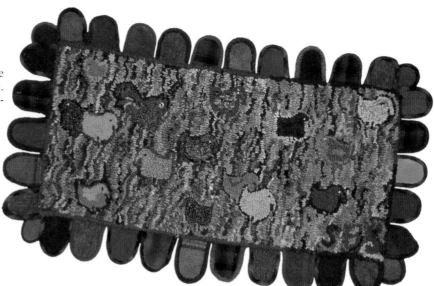

Susie's Chickens. 22" x 38". By Susie Stephenson, Edgecomb, Maine. 2003. "This is a tracing of a flat-backed cookie cutter."

This is Me Riding My Horse. 14" x 13". By Susie Stephenson, Edgecomb, Maine. 2003. "This rug was designed by my son Joseph Hoyt. I think he was in first grade when he gave me the picture and said 'This is me riding my horse.' He was upset that I hooked the words the way he wrote them so I rehooked them. The person is so cute with his one curl and the fact that he has no arms. I think the horse looks like a cat."

Menagerie. 44" x 102" By Susie Stephenson, Edgecomb, Maine. 2004. "This rug is a composite of many of my kids' drawings and artwork. I put them in helter-skelter and dyed up a lot of antique black for the background. This piece took four years to hook."

SHEEP
BY THE JERSEY BAAA'D GIRLS

In the early summer of 2005, a group of new and experienced rug hooking artists who meet regularly in New Jersey decided to do a group rug hooking project. After much discussion about what they wanted to create, the group finally decided on a design of a simple sheep, twelve inches square. All the artists determined the placement of the sheep and how much or how little embellishment to use. They hooked their pieces in private over the summer and unveiled them in the fall of 2005 when they got together again. Featured here are nine of the finished pieces, which now are pillows, table mats, and wall hangings. *Photography by Linda Rae Coughlin.*

Sunny Day Sheep. 12" x 12". By Arline W. Bechtoldt, South Plainfield, New Jersey. 2006.

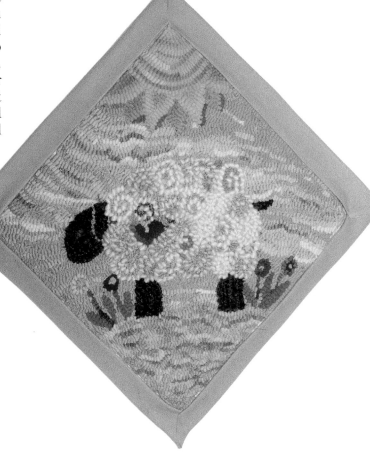

Untitled. 12" x 12". By Janet Bosshard, Lebanon, New Jersey. 2005.

Play the "What If" game. What if I did this, what if I did that?

Watch for the Trees! 12" x 12". By Marilyn Jackson, Basking Ridge, New Jersey. 2005. Pillow.

Sarah's Sheep. 12" x 12". By Claire McDonald, Watchung, New Jersey. 2005.

Isabel. 12" x 12". By Claudia Panizza, Kenilworth, New Jersey. 2005. Pillow.

Baa Baa Black Sheep. 14" x 14". By Amy Tenzer, Short Hills, New Jersey. 2006. Pillow.

Blue Tweed Sheep. 12" x 12". By Ilse R. Vliet, Edison, New Jersey. 2005.

Lambiekins. 12" x 14". By Patricia A. Yost, South Plainfield, New Jersey. 2005.

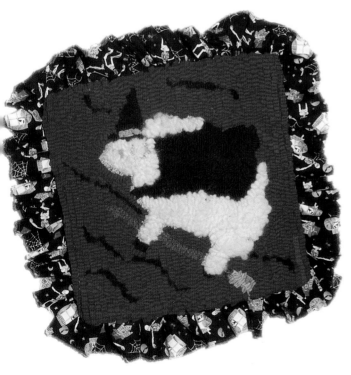

Sheep in Flight. 12" x 12". By Sharon Young, Rahway, New Jersey. 2005.

OTHER ANIMAL RUGS

Some wonderful additional examples of pieces created with an animal theme.

Eagle Eyes. 15" x 19". By Lyle Drier, Waukesha, Wisconsin. 2005. Close-up of a bald eagle. *Courtesy of Lyle Drier.*

Sculpted Butterfly. 12" round. By Patti Ann Finch, Medford, New Jersey. 2003. Footstool. *Courtesy of Patti Ann Finch.*

Sculpted Lizards. 18" round. By Patti Ann Finch, Medford, New Jersey. 2002. Footstool. *Courtesy of Patti Ann Finch.*

Sculpted Frog. 16" round. By Patti Ann Finch, Medford, New Jersey. 2001. Footstool. *Courtesy of Patti Ann Finch.*

Frog Fun. 40" x 24". By Patti Ann Finch, Medford, New Jersey. 2002. *Courtesy of Patti Ann Finch.*

Five Finch Frogs. 41" x 52". By Patti Ann Finch, Medford, New Jersey. 2005. *Courtesy of Patti Ann Finch.*

Hercules. 14" x 12". By Taia L. Harrison, Berkley Heights, New Jersey. 2006. Inspired by her favorite horse. First piece hooked and designed at age twelve. *Photography by Linda Rae Coughlin.*

Lambs' Tongues. 35" x 40". By Joyce Krueger, Waukesha, Wisconsin. 2005. "Adapted from a photo of a painted lamb, this rug was designed with the lambs' tongues facing the center of the motif." *Courtesy of Joyce Krueger.*

Giraffe. 20" x 18". By Karen Maddox, Kerrville, Texas. 2004. "This is a pillow made with all recycled wool. The giraffe has beautiful eyes and long lashes." *Courtesy of Karen Maddox.*

Night Mare. 27" x 21". By Karen Maddox, Kerrville, Texas. 2003. "Using recycled wool, this rug shows how a horse's head might appear at night under a light." *Courtesy of Karen Maddox.*

Mallard Duck. 20" x 26". By Karen Maddox, Kerrville, Texas. 2000. "This is a mallard duck guarding eggs in the nest. Each strip of wool in the grass is a different color." *Courtesy of Karen Maddox.*

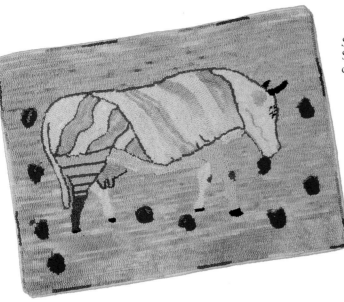

Strawberry Cream. 20" x 27". By Sybil Mercer, Southampton, Ontario, Canada. 2005. Ice cream series #2. *Photography by Fran Sanagan.*

Skim Milk. 20" x 27". By Sybil Mercer, Southampton, Ontario, Canada. 2005. "First piece in my ice cream series. What better way to enjoy luscious ice cream!" *Photography by Fran Sanagan.*

Emperor Penguins at Play - Ice Fishing. 17" x 22". By Julie Robinson, Loudon, New Hampshire. 2005. "This piece was designed for the Hooked in the Mountains Show 'Let's Play.' I thought it would be cute to have the two penguins ice fishing for the fun of it." *Courtesy of Julie Robinson.*

Spotted Turtle. 11" x 11". By Julie Robinson, Loudon, New Hampshire. 2005. Being a wildlife biologist and seeing the beautiful turtles on occasion, Julie is inspired to use the "painted" method of dyeing to give her wool the wetland effect. *Courtesy of Julie Robinson.*

Chapter Three
ARTISTS WITH DISABILITIES

Artists with disabilities often show a rich variety of talents. Thanks to group centers that provide support to these artists, they are increasingly becoming regarded as an active part of the art community. Highlighted in this chapter are examples of some of the wonderful rugs being created at one of these centers, The Ark/LCASC of Bridgewater, Nova Scotia, Canada.

THE ARK / LCASC

Established in 1964, The Ark/Lunenburg County Association for the Specially Challenged, in Canada, provides programs and services for adults with special challenges.

Designer Ellen Balser is one of the artists who comes to The Ark. From an artistic family, she is very pleased to have others hooking her patterns. The Schizophrenic Society of Canada sponsored Ellen to take an art class with an art teacher. She now has a large portfolio and greets Doris Eaton, one of the fiber artists who volunteers at the center each week, with new works of art. Each time Doris arrives at The Ark, she is met by Ellen, who asks Doris if she thinks her new drawings will make a good rug. *Photography courtesy of Doris Eaton.*

What Bugs You. 20" x 24". By Lisa Beck, Bridgewater, Nova Scotia, Canada. 2003. "I like looking at bugs–not touching them–and watching butterflies floating around. I like all different greens. I really like green. I never thought about it before, but I do."

Scenic Nature. 19" x 49". By Lisa Beck, Bridgewater, Nova Scotia, Canada. 2003. Lisa really likes animals. This rug was inspired by an image on a sweatshirt.

Salmon. 18" x 36". By Judy Banfield, Bridgewater, Nova Scotia, Canada. 2002. "My boss asked me to hook a rug of a salmon he caught. It is life-size"

Garden Pond. 20" x 24". By Lisa Beck, Bridgewater, Nova Scotia, Canada. 2002. "It's a frog thing. I really like the color of frogs. I like details, and if you do insects and such, you need to go into detail."

Swan Rug. 15" x 19". By Linda Copeland, Bridgewater, Nova Scotia, Canada. 2004. Designed by Ellen Balser. Ellen says, "I saw this picture of a swan, and I thought it would make a different type of rug."

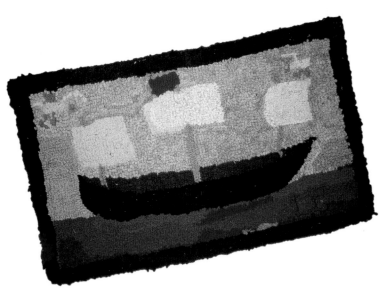

Linda's Boat. 18" x 22". By Linda Copeland, Bridgewater, Nova Scotia, Canada. 2003. "I made this rug because I like boats and seagulls."

Lighthouse. 20" x 20". By Linda Copeland, Bridgewater, Nova Scotia, Canada. 2003.

The Moose on the Weather Lands. 24" x 32". By Linda Copeland, Bridgewater, Nova Scotia, Canada. 2005. Designed by Ellen Balser. Ellen says, "I thought the moose design would make a good rug because of the bright colors I put into it. The moose is near water with wetlands around it."

Bobcat Rug. 22" x 18". By Linda Copeland, Bridgewater, Nova Scotia, Canada. 2004. Designed by Ellen Balser. Ellen says, "I thought kids would like this in their bedroom. I've seen a bobcat at a wildlife park."

Shark Fishing. 29" x 20". By Heather Falkenham, Bridgewater, Nova Scotia, Canada. 2003. Heather saw an article about shark fishing in the local newspaper. She was very impressed and hooked it into a rug.

Hockey in the Thunderstorm. 20" x 16". By Heather Falkenham, Bridgewater, Nova Scotia, Canada. 2002. Hockey is one of Heather's passions.

Dogs and Tulips. 16" x 24". By Heather Falkenham, Bridgewater, Nova Scotia, Canada. 2001. "This is Roxanne's dog. I made this rug in springtime when there were tulips."

Lighthouse Silhouette. 10" x 19". By Pauline Forward, Bridgewater, Nova Scotia, Canada. 2004.

Bluebirds With Nest. 16" x 22". By Pauline Forward, Bridgewater, Nova Scotia, Canada. 2003. Design by Ellen Balser. Ellen notes, when asked about her skills as a designer, "first I wasn't good at drawing birds, but then I had an artist teach me."

Tunor Boat. 10" x 15". By Jean Himmelman, Bridgewater, Nova Scotia, Canada. 2003. Designed by Bruce Colp. Bruce's dad used to go out on tuna fishing boats. They caught a "Tunor" that was 700 pounds, off the coast of Queens. The boat was called UNI (you and I).

Sharks of Florida: Small, Medium and Large. 18" x 12". By Jean Himmelman, Bridgewater, Nova Scotia, Canada. 2002. Designed by Ellen Balser, who says, "Sharks kill people and fish in the water. It is difficult to draw fish compared to other animals."

Path Through the Mountains. 20" x 10". By Jean Himmelman, Bridgewater, Nova Scotia, Canada. 2002. Designed by Ellen Balser. Ellen says, "This was my first rug design. I did it in all different colors. That is all I thought about, using different colors."

Pumpkins. 17" x 27". By Jean Himmelman, Bridgewater, Nova Scotia, Canada. 2004. "This rug was hooked in the fall with many fall leaves added."

Tall House and Horses. 15" x 12". By Jean Himmelman, Bridgewater, Nova Scotia, Canada. 2003. "I like horses but we never had one."

Laundry Day. 10" x 35". By Jean Himmelman, Bridgewater, Nova Scotia, Canada. 2003. "I enjoy hanging out the laundry. There are some codfish on this line too–to dry."

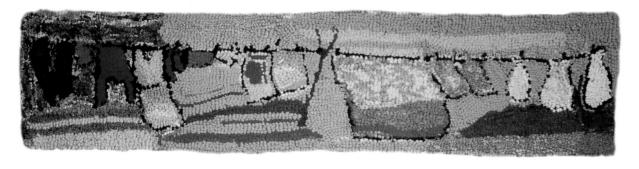

Toy Truck. 23" x 33". By Jean Himmelman, Bridgewater, Nova Scotia, Canada. 2003. "One of the best Christmas presents I ever got was a wooden toy truck my grandfather made for me, just like the one on this rug."

It's Always Windy at Five Houses. 15" x 25". By Jean Himmelman, Bridgewater, Nova Scotia, Canada. 2002. "I grew up at Five Houses right close to the ocean. The clothes on the line blew sideways."

Cats Around the House. 26" x 24". By Jean Himmelman, Bridgewater, Nova Scotia, Canada. 2003. Jean loves cats. On this day, she shows a cat on the fridge, on the bed, in a basket, and one hiding behind the blocks.

Inkwell Story. 24" x 24". By Rosie Leopold, Bridgewater, Nova Scotia, Canada. 2004. Rosie was teased in school by the boys. One day they snuck up on her and put her braids into the inkwell. Her hair had to be cut off. The boys all got detention.

Coastal Fishing Village. 17" x 40". By Darlene Levy, Bridgewater, Nova Scotia, Canada. 2004. "I drew it on a rainy day, then the sun came out and there was a rainbow."

Moose. 15" x 25". By Darlene Levy, Bridgewater, Nova Scotia, Canada. 2001. This pattern was given to Darlene by a friend. She had fun hooking it.

New Ross Farm. 10" x 28". By Darlene Levy, Bridgewater, Nova Scotia, Canada. 2004. New Ross Farm is a working farm museum in Nova Scotia. Darlene grew up one mile from this museum. She has hooked over seventy rugs in the few years she has been at The Ark.

My Grandfather's Copper Shop. 27" x 32". By Darlene Levy, Bridgewater, Nova Scotia, Canada. 2003. "When I grew up, my grandfather took me to his copper shop. He also used to make barrels. I show in the rug the tools he used: a drawknife, a special hammer, and the hoops."

Chicken Farm. 16" x 27". By Darlene Levy, Bridgewater, Nova Scotia, Canada. 2003. "When mother and dad used to have chickens, they would always come into the house. I used to chase them out when I was living at home. A hen lays eggs–she is sitting on her eggs."

Sailboat Scene. 19" x 44". By Darlene Levy, Bridgewater, Nova Scotia, Canada. 2003. "The old people didn't have much food. They needed a garden, and also needed to have food on the boats. They needed fish and vegetables to eat while out on the boats fishing." (Note the long garden on the shore.)

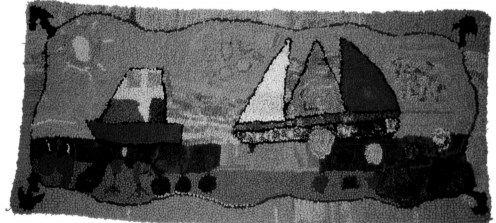

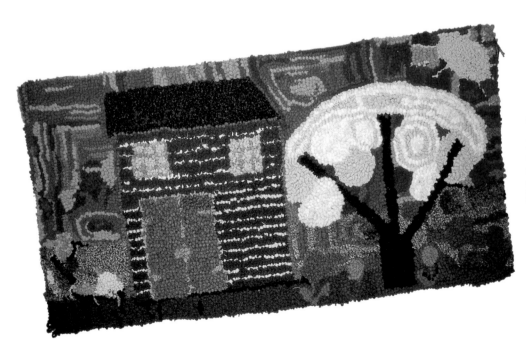

Barn With Apple Blossoms. 15" x 24". By Darlene Levy, Bridgewater, Nova Scotia, Canada. 2003. "My grandfather had a barn with an apple tree right beside it. I remember eating the apples."

Lila is Everybody's Cat. 16" round. By Kenny Mosher, Bridgewater, Nova Scotia, Canada. 2005. "I like to take care of Lila. She climbs up on my lap when I get home and curls up and purrs by my neck." This is Kenny's first rug. He wanted it to have a braided edge, which was added by folks at "The Ark."

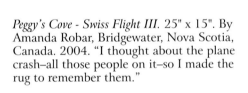

Peggy's Cove - Swiss Flight III. 25" x 15". By Amanda Robar, Bridgewater, Nova Scotia, Canada. 2004. "I thought about the plane crash–all those people on it–so I made the rug to remember them."

Spring. 16" x 22". By Caroline Roellinghoff, Bridgewater, Nova Scotia, Canada. 2005. "Spring makes me think about birds and butterflies."

Port Greville. 21" x 16". By Caroline Roellinghoff, Bridgewater, Nova Scotia, Canada. 2004. "This is my grandfather's place in Port Greville during springtime when the lupines are in bloom."

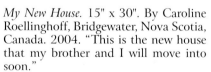

Man Indian. 24" x 19". By Susanne Vienneau, Bridgewater, Nova Scotia, Canada. 2002. An Indian warrior.

My New House. 15" x 30". By Caroline Roellinghoff, Bridgewater, Nova Scotia, Canada. 2004. "This is the new house that my brother and I will move into soon."

Portrait of My Family. 22" x 34". By Susanne Vienneau, Bridgewater, Nova Scotia, Canada. 2004. Susanne's interest in her native heritage started after hearing this story. "Long, long time ago, my mom's mother and father, Cassey Nickerson and Alex Pictou, were 100% pure Indian status. I didn't know my mother was half and half, between 50% to 75% Indian. And then it came down onto her family and we her children knew we had Indian in us. At the time I learned this, I had become very crafty, making my own Indian hooked rugs, just being like my oldest sister who tried to teach me other Indian crafts. That's when I started hooking rugs onto my family heritage background."

My Family Heritage. 22" x 34". By Susanne Vienneau, Bridgewater, Nova Scotia, Canada. 2004. "This rug has my Nanny, Grampy, and Aunt Lena and Uncle Abraham Pictou in it. I also added some Indian designs I found from some petroglyphs in Kejimkujik Park."

Marion Irene Pictou. 24" x 19". By Susanne Vienneau, Bridgewater, Nova Scotia, Canada. 2003. Taken from a photo of Susanne's mother when she wore the same gold gown and peaked cap.

Of My Relations. 23" x 35". By Susanne Vienneau, Bridgewater, Nova Scotia, Canada. 2003. "'Of My Relations' is about where my family lived in the desert. They used to live in a birch bark tent to keep themselves warm over the winter. They played their Indian drums and did their dances around the campfire during the night. They had a newborn baby in a papoose that they were raising. They didn't have much food and could not afford to buy much either."

Turtle and Sheep. 18" x 34". By Patsy Whynot, Bridgewater, Nova Scotia, Canada. 2004. "The grass is green. The turtle is in the grass. The sheep is in the grass. The clouds are in the sky."

By the Sea. 18" x 25". By Patsy Whynot, Bridgewater, Nova Scotia, Canada. 2004. "I like lupine flowers and things found by the seashore."

My Favorite Things. 17" x 28". By Patsy Whynot, Bridgewater, Nova Scotia, Canada. 2003. For this rug, Patsy drew pictures of some of her favorite things: a ball, a ring, a bunny, a ladybug, a banana, and a heart.

Bald Eagle. 24" x 16". By Patsy Whynot, Bridgewater, Nova Scotia, Canada. 2002. Designed by Ellen Balser. Ellen says, "I thought a bald eagle might be something people would be interested in, grown-ups mostly."

Family Rug. 12" x 16". By Patsy Whynot, Bridgewater, Nova Scotia, Canada. 2002. Patsy's parents picking apples in Annapolis Valley.

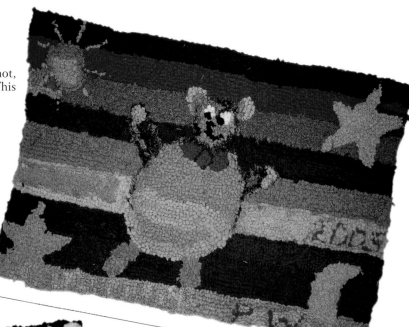

Rainbow Colours. 16" x 23". By Patsy Whynot, Bridgewater, Nova Scotia, Canada. 2005. "This rug is for a child: they like teddy bears."

Pink Piggy. 19" x 23". By Patsy Whynot, Bridgewater, Nova Scotia, Canada. 2002. "No real reason, I wanted to hook a pig. I guess I like pigs"

Hunchback Whale. 20" x 22". By David Wile, Bridgewater, Nova Scotia, Canada. 2004. "I thought it would be a nice different rug with a whale on it. I have seen a big whale in Digby and I have seen a whale at Marine Land in Toronto. They are really big."

Chapter Four
CELEBRATIONS

When we think of a celebration, we are often reminded of a holiday or an occasion to hold up for public acclaim. No matter what the occasion, it is always nice to remember and mark a special event. What better way than with a piece of art!

BIRTH RUGS
BY HAPPY DIFRANZA

Proud grandparents, Happy DiFranza hooked and her husband Steve designed these four birth rugs for each of their four grandchildren.
Photography courtesy of The DiFranzas.

One, Two, Three Rug. 36" x 50". By Happy DiFranza, North Reading, Massachusetts. 2003. "This rug was created in honor of the birth of Jordan Lawrence Terry."

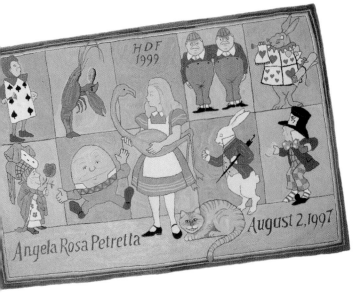

Alice in Wonderland. 38" x 55". By Happy DiFranza, North Reading, Massachusetts. 1999. "The ink drawing of John Tenniel inspired this piece in honor of the birth of Angela Rosa Petretta."

Noah's Ark. 40" x 50". By Happy DiFranza, North Reading, Massachusetts. 1994. "This piece was created in honor of the birth of Domenic Joseph Petretta."

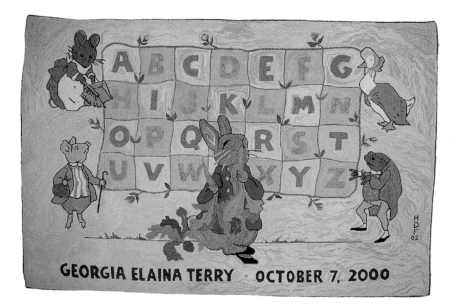

Peter Rabbit Rug. 36" x 52". By Happy DiFranza, North Reading, Massachusetts. 2002. "This piece was created in honor of the birth of Georgia Elaina Terry."

THE US – JAPAN HOOKED RUG EXHIBITION II

Kei Kobayashi, who lives in both New York City, New York and Tokyo, Japan, curated the second international rug hooking exhibit held at the Promenade Gallery in Tokyo, from November 20th to December 9th, 2005. This very successful invitational exhibition was seen by thousands and featured the art of fifteen Japanese and seven American artists.

One of the artists who participated in the exhibit but whose work ("Reminisce") is not featured is John Flournoy. *Photography courtesy of Kei Kobayashi.*

Come and See the Exhibition. 25" x 40". By Kei Kobayashi, NYC, New York. 2005. "All twenty-two participants' names are hooked along with a heart, an observing eye, blessing hand of 'Hearts and Hands' and throwing red paint for my hopes of getting more involved in new ideas. My maximum strength age is 72."

Prosperity, Thrift, Science, and Art. 30" x 45". By Kei Kobayashi, NYC, New York. 2005. "Inspired by a building marker on an old building that read, 'Industry, Thrift, Science, Prosperity, and Art.'"

Ichiro. 22" x 32". By Kazuko Kaneko, Chiba, Japan. 2005. "In celebration of my son's record. I am his biggest fan."

Memorable Summer. 30" x 38". By Kazuko Kaneko, Chiba, Japan. 2005. "I visited my son's camp in 1991 and now he is in college. It is a treasured memory for me."

I Can Hear Music ... 29" x 43". By Kazuko Kawai, Matsudo, Chiba, Japan. 2005.

Cats' Concert II. 29" x 43". By Kazuko Kawai,
Matsudo, Chiba, Japan. 2005.

Flower and Anchor. 17" x 17". By Hiroshi
Ariyoshi, Yokohama, Kanagawa, Japan.
2005. "Made for my husband who retired as
CEO of Mitsubishi Heavy Industry, Ltd."

My Family I. 30" x 36". By Kumiko Fujita,
Kumagae, Saitama, Japan. 2005.

My Family II. 30" x 41". By Kumiko Fujita,
Kumagae, Saitama, Japan. 2005.

From the Age of Dinosaurs to Present I.
24" x 30". By Mitsue Fukuda, Chiba,
Japan. 2005.

*From the Age of Dinosaurs to Present
II.* 24" x 30". By Mitsue Fukuda,
Chiba, Japan. 2005.

Who Owns the Planet? 32" x 40". By
Setsuko Fukuda, Kokubuji, Japan. 2005.
"Concerning ecocide."

Sun Flower. 28" x 26". By Setsuko Fukuda, Kokubuji,
Japan. 2005. "All should look forward to the sun."

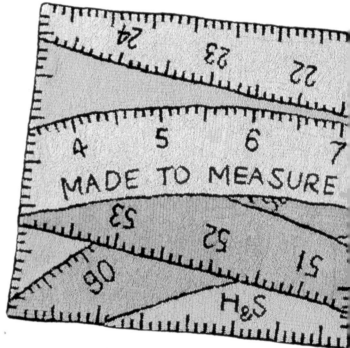

Made To Measure. 24" x 26". By Keiko Hara, Tokyo,
Japan. 2005. Designed by Hiromi Sakamoto and
hooked by Keiko Hara. Both are designers working at
fashion maker "Homespun" in Japan.

Needlework. 29" x 25". By Eriko Keino, Tachikawa,
Japan. 2005. "I wanted to express my rug as an
embroidery."

Welcome Rug. 32" x 40". By Hiromi Klyama, Tokyo, Japan. 2005.

Furisode – A Long Sleeved Kimono. 47" x 30". By Utsumi Klyama, Tokyo, Japan. 2005. This kimono was made for Utsumi's eighteenth birthday celebration ceremony. Long sleeve kimonos are usually worn before marriage.

Petals II. 25" x 34". By Kazuko Kobayashi, Tokyo, Japan. 2005. "I found that geometric designs are more difficult than free hand designs."

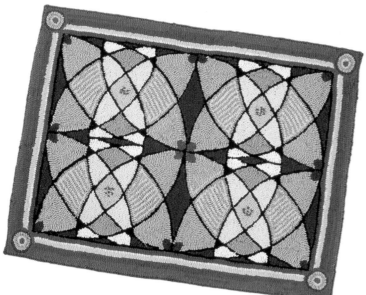

Petals I. 21" x 27". By Kazuko Kobayashi, Tokyo, Japan. 2005. "I wanted to try a geometric design."

Flying Cranes. 24" x 30". By Haruyo Murata, Tokyo, Japan. 2005.

Honeycomb. 23" x 24". By Haruyo Murata, Tokyo, Japan. 2005.

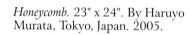

Mixed. 29" x 44". By Hiromi Murata, Tokyo, Japan. 2005.

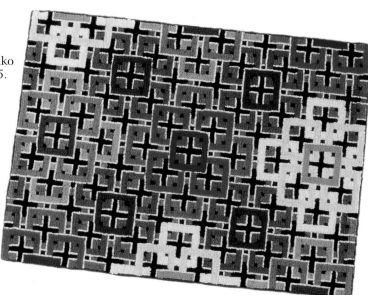

Hydrangea. 29" x 41". By Mitsuko Mochizuki, Tokyo, Japan. 2005.

Rainbow and Flowers. 25" x 29". By Mitsuko Mochizuki, Tokyo, Japan. 2005.

Cape Cod Cat. 23" x 39". By Marilyn Bottjer, Eastchester, New York. 2005.

Pin Wheel. 28" x 46". By Liz Albert Fay, Sandy Hook, Connecticut. 2005.

America, America. 31" x 32". By Alice Rudell, New York City, New York. 2005.

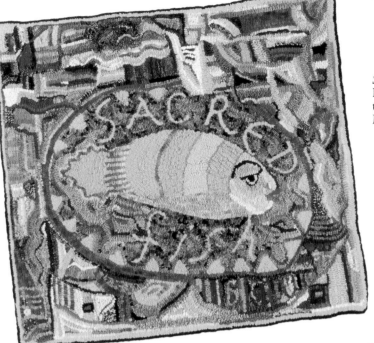

Sacred Fish. 33" x 30". By Burma Cassidy, Rochester, Vermont. 2004. "Inspired by my travels to Three Rivers Petroglyphs in New Mexico."

Afternoon Delight. 30" x 33". By Michele Micarelli, New Haven, Connecticut. 2004. A self-portrait.

Rhus Radicans. 21" x 16". By Linda Rae Coughlin, Warren, New Jersey. 2003. "This piece looks at gossip, and how like poison ivy it can be very dangerous."

Chapter Five
THE CIRCUS

The theme of a circus conjures up endless design ideas, as you can see from the many creative pieces showcased in this chapter.

CIRCUS TRAIN

The idea of a "Circus" or "Under the Big Top" was chosen as the theme for the 2000 "Hooked in the Mountains" rug show, which is put on each year by the Green Mountain Rug Hooking Guild of Vermont. In conjunction with this theme, the idea of the entire guild participating in a group project to create a circus train was also conceived.

Each artist who took part in the project was given a piece of rug warp and asked to design a rug measuring 15" x 18". The only design restrictions were that each rug would have to have two train wheels plus a train hitch hooked at the front and back of the piece. This would give a unified look to the entire train when it was hung as a collection to form the circus train. The artists were free to design their pieces any way they chose and were asked to donate their finished pieces to the Green Mountain Guild.

Patty Yoder wrote about this train, "The cars reflect a diversity of hooking styles, subject choices, and finishing techniques. What holds the cars together is their whimsy and playfulness. For some, this was their first experience designing a rug. Many people described the pleasure of experimenting with colors and designs that were different from their normal style. Independently, many artists embellished their rugs with unique and sparkling additions. The results were spectacular."

After the rug show that year, the "Circus Train" was seen as an important collection that could help to promote the art of rug hooking. It was purchased by Patty Yoder, then President of the Green Mountain Rug Guild, who subsequently lent it out to be used as an educational tool by any of the many rug hooking guilds and nonprofit organizations around the country. Featured here are sixty-two of the rugs that were part of the exhibit.

One of the artists who participated in the "Circus Train" project but whose piece did not appear in this section is Burma Cassidy.

Photography courtesy of Ramsey Yoder.

Circus Train Engine. By Jule Marie Smith, Ballston Spa, New York. 2000.

Tiger. By Ann Winterling, Concord, New Hampshire. 2000.

Elephant on Main St. By Anne-Marie W. Littenberg, Burlington, Vermont. 2000.

All Aboard. By Barbara Bessette, Danville, Vermont. 2000.

Moonlight Ride. By Barbara Bessette, Danville, Vermont. 2000.

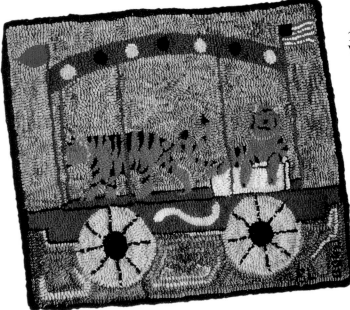

Two Tigers. By Barbara Ludwig, Belmont, Vermont. 2000. Designed by Jean Ellis.

Summer 2000 Circus Show, Mt. Tremblant, Québec. By Barbara Lukas, Ottawa, Ontario, Canada. 2000.

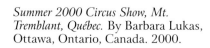

The Zebra Car. By Betty Bouchard, Richmond, Vermont. 2000.

Basic Food Groups. By Beverly Delnicki, Wheelock, Vermont. 2000.

Balloons. By Celeste Bessette, Manchester, New Hampshire. 2000.

Peta, The Clown. By Davey DeGraff, Hinesburg, Vermont. 2000.

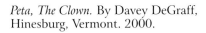

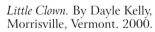

Little Clown. By Dayle Kelly, Morrisville, Vermont. 2000.

Giraffe. By Deborah Kelley, Shoreham, Vermont. 2000. Designed by Beverly Conway.

The Amazing Zeus. By Debra Boudrieau, Bellows Falls, Vermont. 2000.

B is for Bonnie, Who Does a Daily Balancing Act. By Patty Yoder, Tinmouth, Vermont. 2000.

Four Circus Elephants. By Diane S. Kelly, Dorset, Vermont. 2000.

See Baby Betty. By Diane Phillips, Fairport, New York. 2000.

The Blue Elephants. By George Kahnle & Dick Labarge, Victory Mills, New York. 2000.

Cotton Candy. By Donna Lee Beaudoin, Hinesburg, Vermont. 2000.

Tuxedo, Frankie and Buttercup. By Elizabeth Morgan, Wallingford, Vermont. 2000.

Circus Lion. By Ellen Gonnet,
Fayston, Vermont. 2000.

Lion. By Fern Strong, East Hartford,
Connecticut. 2000. Designed by
Beverly Conway.

Ben. By Frank Hanchett, Francestown,
New Hampshire. 2000.

Clown on Two-Headed Cow. By Gail Duclos Lapierre, Shelburne, Vermont. 2000.

Betty the Beelady. By Heather Burns, Chuckatuck, Virginia. 2000.

Giraffe. By Jean Baldyga, Coventry, Connecticut. 2000. Designed by Beverly Conway.

Tigers Rule. By Joan Dubois-Frey, Cornwell, Vermont. 2000.

Fur Lady. By Joan Stocker, Kittery Point, Maine. 2000.

Elephant. By Jo-Ann Millen, Boxford, Massachusetts. 2000.

Cops and Robbers. By Joanne Miller, Canaan, New Hampshire. 2000.

Calliope. By John Woodard, Greenwich, Connecticut. 2000.

Top Cat. By Judith Osler Phillips, Boston, Massachusetts. 2000.

The Two Lions. By Judy Quintman, Wilmington, North Carolina. 2000.

Painted Pony. By Julie Rogers, Huntington, Vermont. 2000.

Gypsy. By Kathleen Patten, Hinesburg, Vermont. 2000.

Circus Bear. By Kim Dubay, No. Yarmouth, Maine. 2000.

Circus Clown. By Linda Potvin, Mount Holly, Vermont. 2000.

Circus Fairy. By Linda Rae Coughlin, Warren, New Jersey. 2000.

CIRCUS FAIRY

Circus Tent. By Loretta Bucceri,
Danby, Vermont. 2000.

Le Cirque Leo. By Lory Doolittle,
Mt. Holly, Vermont. 2000.

The Clowns. By Margot Powell, Barnard,
Vermont. 2000.

Not Endangered Species Anymore. By Mary Sargent, Johnson, Vermont. 2000.

Flora, Elegant Elephant. By Nancy Bachand, Vergennes, Vermont. 2000.

Buster the Wonder Dog. By Nancy Phillips, North Fayston, Vermont. 2000.

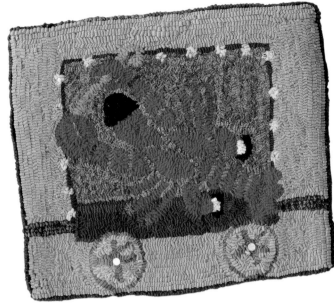

Lobster in a Trap. By Natacha Pouech, Hinesburg, Vermont. 2000.

Exotic Birds. By Norma Batastini, Glen Ridge, New Jersey. 2000.

Ellie. By Pamela Carter, Bristol, Vermont. 2000. Designed by Beverly Conway.

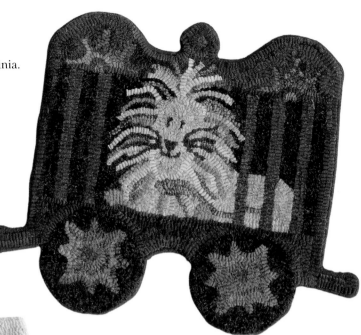

Lion. By Pat Cross, Charlottesville, Virginia. 2000.

Circus Camel. By Peggy Stanilonis, Vergennes, Vermont. 2000.

Misha. By Polly Alexander, Essex Junction, Vermont. 2000.

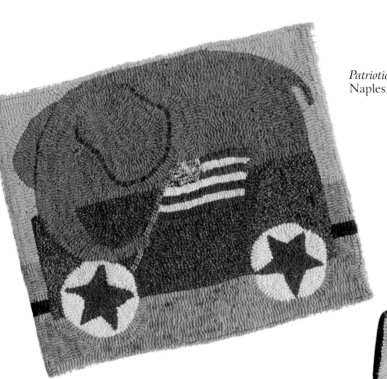

Patriotic Elephant. By Polly Minick,
Naples, Florida. 2000.

Cleo, The Queen of Denial. By Rae Reynolds
Harrell, Hinesburg, Vermont. 2000.

Oom Pah Pah Man. By Rae Reynolds
Harrell, Hinesburg, Vermont. 2000.

Circus Tiger. By Shirley H. Zandy, Tinmouth, Vermont. 2000.

Peanuts. By Susan Longchamp, West Burke, Vermont. 2000.

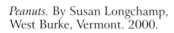

Clowns and Lion. By Sue Hommel, Rutland, Vermont. 2000.

Circus Horse. By Susan Gingras, Weybridge, Vermont. 2000.

Fun Clowns. By Susan Mackey, Tinmouth, Vermont. 2000.

The Pink Elephant. By Susan L. Smidt, Salem, Massachusetts. 2000.

Giraffe in a Circus Wagon. By
Suzanne Dirmaier, Waterbury
Center, Vermont. 2000.

Circus Box Car. By Trinka Parker,
Hinesburg, Vermont. 2000.

The End. By Laurilyn Wiles,
Hinesburg, Vermont. 2000.

OTHER CIRCUS RUGS

Featured here are some examples of other pieces created with a circus theme.

Lion with Monkey. 17" x 20". By Maryanne Lincoln, Wrentham, Massachusetts. 2003. Featured in a "Recipes from the Dye Kitchen" article in *Rug Hooking Magazine.* *Photography by Linda Rae Coughlin.*

Car Full of Clowns. 19" x 26". By Maryanne Lincoln, Wrentham, Massachusetts. 2002. Featured in a "Recipes from the Dye Kitchen" article in *Rug Hooking Magazine. Photography by Linda Rae Coughlin.*

Baby Elephant. 14" x 16". By Maryanne Lincoln, Wrentham, Massachusetts. 2001. Featured in a "Recipes from the Dye Kitchen" article in *Rug Hooking Magazine. Photography by Linda Rae Coughlin.*

Uncle Sam on Stilts. 18" x 10". By Maryanne Lincoln, Wrentham, Massachusetts. 1995. Featured in a "Recipes from the Dye Kitchen" article in *Rug Hooking Magazine. Photography by Linda Rae Coughlin.*

Bear on Unicycle. 19" x 10". By Maryanne Lincoln, Wrentham, Massachusetts. 2001. Featured in a "Recipes from the Dye Kitchen" article in *Rug Hooking Magazine. Photography by Linda Rae Coughlin.*

Sea Lion. 14" x 10". By Maryanne Lincoln, Wrentham, Massachusetts. 2003. Featured in a "Recipes from the Dye Kitchen" article in *Rug Hooking Magazine. Photography by Linda Rae Coughlin.*

Jay's Tiger. 22" x 19". By Matilda K. Weeks,
Port Murray, New Jersey. 2004. *Photography
by Linda Rae Coughlin.*

Circus Tiger. 48" x 60". By Arne Nyen,
Stockholm, Wisconsin. 1998. Tufted
rug commissioned for the Shriner's
Headquarters, Atlanta, Georgia. *Courtesy of Arne Nyen.*

Chapter Six
FACES AND PORTRAITS

Among the most available, but not always the most willing, subjects for creating art are the self and others. In the past, very few rugs featured the human body as a subject, but today you will find numerous artists using this as a main subject and theme in many of their rugs.

SELF-PORTRAITS BY THE NINE

Anne-Marie W. Littenberg, a member of the group, writes:

Rug hookers have tender hearts, and when they are asked to evaluate each other's work, their feedback is universally positive. The late Patty Yoder posed the question, 'How will we ever learn and grow if even our closest rug-hooking friends provide only accolades for our work?' She was dedicated to bringing the art of rug hooking to a higher level, and she understood that this required hooked rugs to undergo the rigors of critical study and evaluation that has always been applied to the world of 'fine art.' Rug hookers need to lift their focus above the world of crafts and patterns, and the art-viewing public must be educated to understand that hooked rugs can be a rich source of moving artistic expression.

With this in mind, Patty invited a handful of fiber-arts colleagues to join her on a journey of study. The group decided to focus its efforts on creating an original body of work through mutual support, nurturing, sharing of knowledge, and critical evaluation. Informally calling themselves "Nine," they strive to have their work recognized at a national level, beyond the boundaries of the world of rug hooking. The group works together to hone skills, keeping in mind individual ranges of style and experience. They have worked on the art and craft of critiquing and evaluating their work, and honing their technical and artistic skills.

The nine self-portraits were completed to serve as the group's identifying logo for exhibition. The challenge was to create self-portraits that, while not photo-realistic, represented each artist's style of expression. In addition, each self-portrait bears a strong resemblance to its respective artist. If you put the group in a room together, you can easily identify which artist created which piece.

The group evolves as art evolves. Having worked on skills-related challenges, the group also participates in exhibits–individually and jointly. They take field trips to museums together, study art outside their medium, and bring in outside artists to provide them with personalized instruction.

With the passing of Patty Yoder, and with Burma Cassidy leaving because of other commitments, the group presently consists of seven members.
Each portrait measures 14" square.
Photography by Rae Harrell.

Burma. By Burma Cassidy, Rochester, Vermont. 2005.

Molly. By Molly Dye, Jacksonville, Vermont. 2005.

Rae. By Rae Reynolds Harrell, Hinesburg, Vermont. 2005.

Barbara. By Barbara Held, Tinmouth, Vermont. 2005.

Diane. By Diane S. Kelly, Dorset, Vermont. 2005.

Anne-Marie. By Anne-Marie W. Littenberg,
Burlington, Vermont. 2005.

Diane. By Diane Phillips, Fairport, New York. 2005.

Jule Marie. By Jule Marie Smith, Ballston Spa, New York. 2005.

Patty. By Patty Yoder, Tinmouth, Vermont. 2005.

THE COLOR OF MY MIND

These seven self-portraits were created by a group of artists who worked with fiber artist Rae Harrell in January of 2005. The group met at the home of Jill Cooper of Riverdale, Georgia, for a three-day workshop. When an unexpected ice and snowstorm hit, they had no heat or electricity for two days. The group created these pieces with only the light and heat from the fire in Jill's fireplace.

Out of My Mind. 22" x 25". By Kathie Meyers, Fayetteville, Georgia. 2005. *Courtesy of Kathie Meyers.*

Eve Transformed. 32" x 24". By Linda Tindal Davis, Atlanta, Georgia. 2005. *Courtesy of Linda Tindal Davis.*

I Can. 25" x 24". By Jennie Adcock, Newman, Georgia. 2005. *Courtesy of Jennie Adcock.*

Straight Forward. 24" x 20". By Nancy Ratliff, Conyers, Georgia. 2005. *Courtesy of Nancy Ratliff.*

The Middle Age. 14" x 11". By Carolyn Folsom, Cumming, Georgia. 2005. *Courtesy of Carolyn Folsom.*

The Dreamer. 24" x 28". By Laura Strawn, Jonesboro, Georgia. 2005. *Courtesy of Laura Strawn.*

The Colors of My Mind. 40" x 27". By Jill Cooper, Riverdale, Georgia. 2005. *Courtesy of Jill Cooper.*

FACE MASKS

The fiber study group "Les Hookeuses du Bor'de'lo" of Shediac, New Brunswick, Canada explored the concept of faces as masks. Featured here are five masks from this group's study project. *Photography by Christian Ouellet.*

George. 15" x 12". By Grace Ward, Grande-Digue, New Brunswick, Canada. 2004.

African Mask. 20" x 15". By Line Godbout, Shediac, New Brunswick, Canada. 2004.

Variation on O'Keeffe. 18" x 18". By Lynne Ciacco, Hillsborough, New Brunswick, Canada. 2005. "This mask of sorts is based on the O'Keeffe painting 'Cow's Skull, Red White and Blue' (1930). Where O'Keeffe uses a cow's skull from the dry desert, I have used a bird's skull (possibly from a duck) to denote the abundant shores of New Brunswick, Canada."

Mask With a Saw. 25" x 17". By Gisèle Léger Drapeau, Shediac, New Brunswick, Canada. 2005. Inspired by an old saw, this three-dimensional mask was hooked on chicken wire.

3D Mask With Eyes. 24" x 20". By Gisèle Léger Drapeau, Shediac, New Brunswick, Canada. 2004. Hooked into a screen-like material formed into a face using scrap fabric, dog dreadlocks, fur, loopy ear rings and ceramic eyes.

A FEW MORE PORTRAIT RUGS

More exciting and beautifully executed rugs featuring the human body as the main subject matter.

Esther. 50" x 35". By Patty Yoder, Tinmouth, Vermont. 2003. Esther Knipe, Patty's dear friend and rug hooking mentor. *Photography by Linda Rae Coughlin.*

Noah's Ark. 13" x 15". By Susan Andreson, Newport Beach, California. 2005. "Grandpa John (my husband) and our first-born grandson Sam, discovering the joys of the ark." *Courtesy of Susan Andreson.*

Dress Up. 29" x 23". By Susan Mackey, Tinmouth, Vermont. 2005. "Reproduced from a favorite photograph of our children Jessie and Liam. It was taken in 1982 during an afternoon of play. This rug was a gift for Liam in memory of Jessie who died in 1995." *Courtesy of Susan Mackey.*

Emily's Red Gown. 24" x 18". By Janet Williams, Skillman, New Jersey. 1999. Adapted from a photograph of Janet's daughter Emily, at her senior prom in 1998. *Courtesy of Janet Williams.*

My Madonna. 23" x 23". By Gisèle Léger Drapeau, Shediac, New Brunswick, Canada. 2000. This piece was completely hooked on the day Gisèle's mother was diagnosed with cancer, and she put the last stitch in the piece the day of her burial. It has since accompanied friends and other family members on difficult journeys. *Courtesy of Gisèle Léger Drapeau.*

Chapter Seven
FAMILY AND FRIENDS

The ties we have to our families and friends seem to be a common and desirable theme when designing rugs.

RELATIVES THROUGH THE YEARS BY JUDITH C. CREAMER

Judith Crawford Creamer of Melbourne, Florida, is relatively new to rug hooking, but has created this wonderful collection of pieces having to do with her family. Judith was Regent of the Fort Seven Chapter, Severna Park, Maryland NSDAR. She is also an associate member of the Philip Perry Chapter, Coca, Florida NSDAR. She has won many awards for her rugs and they have been displayed at the Flag House in Baltimore, Maryland, Quiet Waters State Park, Annapolis, Maryland, and Montpelier Art Center. *Photography courtesy of Judith C. Creamer.*

One Potato Two Potato. 15" x 18". By Judith Crawford Creamer, Melbourne, Florida. 2002. Judith's aunts and uncles playing One Potato in 1913 on the Crawford Farm in Clark County, Arkansas.

The Kiss. 17" x 12". By Judith Crawford Creamer, Melbourne, Florida. 2001. This piece shows Nolan Crawford and Lois Reagan, Judith's parents, in 1937.

What the Shepherd Family Does. 20" x 19". By Judith Crawford Creamer, Melbourne, Florida. 2002. This rug shows Judith's daughter and her family, the Shepherds, involved in their interests. Kyle raises butterflies. Brenda holds a shepherd's crook showing how she keeps the family pulled together, Jim holds the scales of justice, depicting his profession of law and his ability to balance the family dynamics. In the scales are Duke basketballs, as both parents hold degrees from Duke University. Jake is wearing a shirt that shows his love of action figures. A sheep relaxes close to the Shepherd family.

The Life of Moses Helms. 30" x 36". By Judith Crawford Creamer, Melbourne, Florida. 2004. The Life of Moses Helms (1814-1883) begins at 2:00 o'clock and moves counter clockwise around the rug. He follows in the footsteps of his father, Joel, who was a Primitive Baptist Minister. They were all members of the High Hill Primitive Baptist Church in North Carolina until he and his mother and father were (excommunicated) kicked out. Moses' wife and two children met them as they fell into the wagon. They moved to Alabama where Moses again became active in the Primitive Baptist Church. His first wife died and he married his second wife the next day. They moved to Florida and he died while living on Alligator Creek. His profession of newspaper producer is depicted in the upper left corner. He is the great-grand-father of Judith Creamer.

A Doctor Sneaking Some Fishing Time. 23" x 21". By Judith Crawford Creamer, Melbourne, Florida. 2005. "Dr. Luther Reagan enjoying his favorite leisure time activity in the 1950s. Yes, he always wore a tie."

Praising the Newborn Child in 1922. 19" x 11". By Judith Crawford Creamer, Melbourne, Florida. 2005. Judith's great-grandmother holding her newborn grandchild with the jealous siblings at her feet in 1922.

FRIENDSHIP RUGS I & II BY THE COLONIAL RUG HOOKERS

Stacy LeCure designed a basic tree pattern for her guild members, so that they could each create a friendship rug for an exhibit featuring series rugs, put on by Colonial Rug Hookers of Northern Virginia. The rugs in this series are variations of Stacy's deciduous tree: bark, foliage, blossoms, fruit, setting, and background color. Technique and materials were left to the discretion and imagination of each artist. The first series was completed in 2000 and the second in 2004/2005.

Friendship Series #1. 24" x 26". By Val Carter, Springfield, Virginia. 2000. Courtesy of Val Carter.

Friendship Series #1. 22" x 26". By Ann Campany, Vienna, Virginia. 2000. Courtesy of Ann Campany.

Friendship Series #1. 27" x 30". By Dorothy Gorham, Lorton, Virginia. 2000. Courtesy of Dorothy Gorham.

Friendship Series #2 Samplers of Life. 24" x 28".
By June Britton, Prescott Valley, Arizona. 2004.
"Heart design was chosen because of patriotic
feelings after 9/11/01." *Courtesy of June Britton.*

Friendship Series #2. 25" x 30". By Stacy R. LeCure,
Bristow, Virginia. 2003. *Courtesy of Stacy R. LeCure.*

Friendship Series #2 Old Friends.
23" x 28". By Kathy Meyer,
Chantilly, Virginia. 2004. Rug is
bordered with a friendship quote
by Thomas Jefferson. *Courtesy of
Kathy Meyer.*

Friendship Series #2. 24" x 28". By Barbara Personette, Fairfax, Virginia. 2005. *Courtesy of Barbara Personette.*

Friendship Series #2. 23" x 28". By Terri Schaefer, Leesburg, Virginia. 2005. *Courtesy of Terri Schaefer.*

Friendship Series #2. 25" x 29". By Mary B. Tycz, Falls Church, Virginia. 2004. "The terra cotta red and black border is 4 1/2" wide and includes the words 'Colonial Rug Hookers Guild' in the top border and 'Newbie's Magic Carpet' in the bottom border." *Courtesy of Mary B. Tycz.*

HUDSON VALLEY FRIENDSHIP RUGS

In 2000, a group of rug hookers from Hudson Valley, New York decided to make friendship rugs after seeing, and being inspired, by some rugs done by a rug hooking group from New Jersey. After determining how many people would participate in the challenge, they designed their own rugs, incorporating as many 4" squares as there were people participating. Eighteen people participated in the project, with twelve of them featured here. The squares could be placed anywhere in the rug. Many centered them with an originally designed border; others had the squares around the border and a design in the center. Most people filled the squares on the other rugs with the same design, using different colors and placement. In the end, all the rugs ended up looking very different from each other. *Photography by Roya Zarrehparver.*

Friendship Rug. 26" x 20". By Mary Raymond Alenstein, Briarcliff Manor, New York. 2000.

Friendship Rug. 23" x 27". By Barbara Boll-Ingber, Ossining, New York. 2000.

Friendship Rug. 24" x 33". By Marilyn Bottjer,
Eastchester, New York. 2000.

Friendship Rug. 24" x 30". By Qing Fan-Dollinger,
Croton, New York. 2000.

Friendship Rug. 16" x 25". By Melissa London
Glickman, Croton, New York. 2000.

Friendship Rug. 21" x 28". By Renee Curci Ivanoff,
Croton, New York. 2000.

Friendship Rug. 24" x 26". By Joyce Kapadia, Ossining, New York. 2000.

Friendship Rug. 23" x 30". By Laurie M. Ling, Croton, New York. 2000.

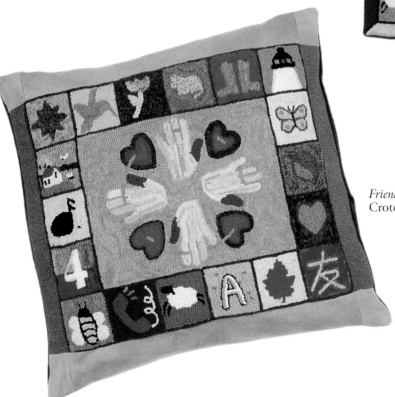

Friendship Rug. 24" x 28". By Andrea Naitove, Croton, New York. 2000.

Friendship Rug. 18" x 29". By Nancy Oppedisano, Ossining, New York. 2000.

Friendship Rug. 17" x 28". By Robin Schwamb, Croton, New York. 2000.

Friendship Rug. 18" x 29". By Diane R. Skalak, Croton, New York. 2000.

FAMILY MEMORIES
BY RUTH HENNESSEY

Ruth Hennessey of Walworth, New York, has created some beautiful family memories in this collection of five rugs. *Photography courtesy of Ruth Hennessey.*

Dad. 15" x 11". By Ruth Hennessey, Walworth, New York. 2001. "My dad–circa 1930."

We Are Family. 16" x 15". By Ruth Hennessey, Walworth, New York. 2000. "Caricatures of my family, including sisters and brothers in-law."

Connor and Sadie. 14" x 11". By Ruth Hennessey, Walworth, New York. 2001.

Hannah and Kids. 14" x 11". By Ruth Hennessey, Walworth, New York. 2003. "Adapted from old family photo circa 1946."

Grandkids. 14" x 11". By Ruth Hennessey, Walworth, New York. 2006. "My grandkids."

OUR FAMILY
BY DANIELLE OUELLET

Danielle Ouellet of New Brunswick, Canada created this wonderful series of four rugs inspired by drawings made by her two children of some of their family members. She writes about her rugs, "though I have no qualms selling my other artwork, when it comes to my hooked tapestries, parting with them is extremely difficult for they become a part of me and my family's history."

Photography by Christian Ouellet.

Dad. 17" x 17". By Danielle Ouellet, Grande-Digue, New Brunswick, Canada. 2002. Inspired by a drawing done by Danielle's five-year-old son. Hooked with t-shirts.

The Four Sisters. 30" x 40". By Danielle Ouellet, Grande-Digue, New Brunswick, Canada. 2000. Inspired by a drawing done by Danielle's five-year-old daughter. Hooked with t-shirts.

Feel the Love. 30" x 40". By Danielle Ouellet, Grande-Digue, New Brunswick, Canada. 2003. Inspired by a drawing done by Danielle's five-year-old daughter. Hooked with t-shirts.

OTHER FAMILY AND FRIEND RUGS

Shown here are some additional rugs with the theme of families and friends.

Cheats Rug. 18" x 24". By Susan Andreson, Newport Beach, California. 2001. "Robert, Bob Cheatley AKA 'Cheats' is our guardian angel. He is a former pro football player who plays basketball, loves old cars, and is a shining star in many ways." *Courtesy of Susan Andreson.*

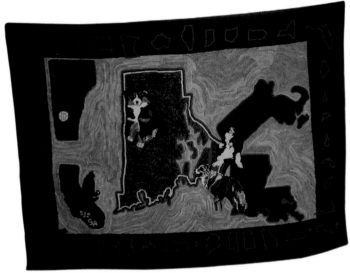

Jennifer's Life Up to Purchasing Her First Home. 24" x 36". By Susan Andreson, Newport Beach, California. 2000. "The center of the rug shows the places she has lived and the things that are important to her." *Courtesy of Susan Andreson.*

Playing at the "Y". 19" x 24". By Judy Dodds, Waitsfield, Vermont. 2005. "This piece was inspired by a photograph of my son and some of the lady board members of the YMCA all doing the 'can-can' at a benefit concert he attended." *Courtesy of Judy Dodds.*

The Tournament. 20" x 68". By Liz Albert Fay, Sandy Hook, Connecticut. 1999. "Inspired by a soccer tournament where, in an effort to occupy my young daughter, we started writing down all the words of encouragement we heard parents yelling out to their children during the soccer games." *Collection of Joan and Martin Messinger.*

Foundation of Our Family. 32" x 48". By Barb Nonnewitz, Aurora, Ontario, Canada. 2004. "The foundation blocks show the care, favorite foods, hobbies, and my brothers and me skinny dipping in the lake. Also shown are hot breakfasts, winter sports and my mother, Sybil Mercer, who is the angel in the center." *Photography by Fran Sanagan.*

Music. 31" x 27". By Karen Maddox, Kerrville, Texas. 2001. This piece was inspired by the fact that my daughter layed the flute, my son played the guitar, and I played the iano." *Courtesy of Karen Maddox.*

Brindiamo con Rosa. 29" x 48". By Alice Rudell, New York City, New York. 2002. "We traveled to Italy with Rosa for many years. This is a toast to her, her horse Patrick, and to the wonderful times we had together." *Courtesy of Alice Rudell.*

Grandkids at the Beach. 15" x 27". By Judy Quintman, Wilmington, North Carolina. 2004. When Judy's grandchildren arrive at her house for a visit the first thing they ask is, "can we go to the beach now?" She had fun thinking of them while creating this piece. *Courtesy of Judy Quintman.*

Knitting. 37" x 51". By Alice Rudell, New York City, New York. 2000. "My mother was a great knitter. This piece shows her in her den on the blue leather sofa. The border is a rendition of the fabric that upholstered the chairs in the room. There is a bowl of M&Ms on the table; this bowl was always full." *Courtesy of Alice Rudell.*

Sisters. 15" x 13". By Paige Osborn Stoep, Lyons, New York. 2002. "This piece was inspired by my two beautiful sisters, Cynthia and Leslie, and the song 'Here I am Lord.'" *Courtesy of Paige Osborn Stoep.*

Snakes Too! 37" x 29". By Sharon L. Townsend, Altoona, Iowa. 2002. Inspired by Noah's Ark. *Courtesy of Sharon L. Townsend.*

"M" is for Maggie. 22" x 18". By Debbie Walsh, Cranford, New Jersey. 2003. Designed by Debbie's daughter Maggie and hooked by Debbie. *Courtesy of Debbie Walsh.*

Mallard Family. 24" x 37". By Janet Williams, Skillman, New Jersey. 2004. Design by Jane McGown Flynn. *Courtesy of Janet Williams.*

Little Shell Seeker. 10" x 13". By Peg Irish & Ann Winterling, Madberry & Concord, New Hampshire. 2004. Collaboration piece designed for the League of New Hampshire 2004 Craftsmen exhibit entitled, "Yours, Mine and Ours." *Courtesy of Linda Rae Coughlin.*

The House in Rhinebeck. 22" x 31". By Ann Winterling, Concord, New Hampshire. 1993. This rug shows Ann as a toddler, circa 1935, at a favorite children's home in New York State. *Photography by Dwayne Bailey.*

Self Portrait With Memories. 24" x 36". By Ann Winterling, Concord, New Hampshire. 2000. A scene of Ann leaning against an old oak tree gazing over her grandparents' and Aunt Helen's farm. Vignettes of important memories are tucked into the roots. *Photography by Dwayne Bailey.*

Garden of the Seven Sisters. 33" x 53". By Gail Ferdinando, Pittstown, New Jersey. 2005. Designed by Gail's step-mom Judy Quintman. Three rugs were hooked–one by Gail, one by Judy, and one by Gail's sister Debbie Walsh. *Courtesy of Gail Ferdinando.*

Garden of the Seven Sisters. 33" x 53". By Judy Quintman, Wilmington, North Carolina. 2004. This rug was drawn by Judy and given to each of her two step-daughters (twins) for their birthday. All three would hook the same rug. They decided that they wouldn't talk about how they were hooking their pieces, but would wait until they were finished to see how they turned out. They were all very surprised to see that the three rugs looked very similar. " It was a fun family project." *Courtesy of Judy Quintman.*

Garden of the Seven Sisters. 33" x 53". By Debbie Walsh, Cranford, New Jersey. 2004. Designed by Debbie's step-mom Judy Quintman. Three rugs were hooked–one by Debbie, one by Judy, and one by Debbie's sister Gail Ferdinando. *Courtesy of Debbie Walsh.*

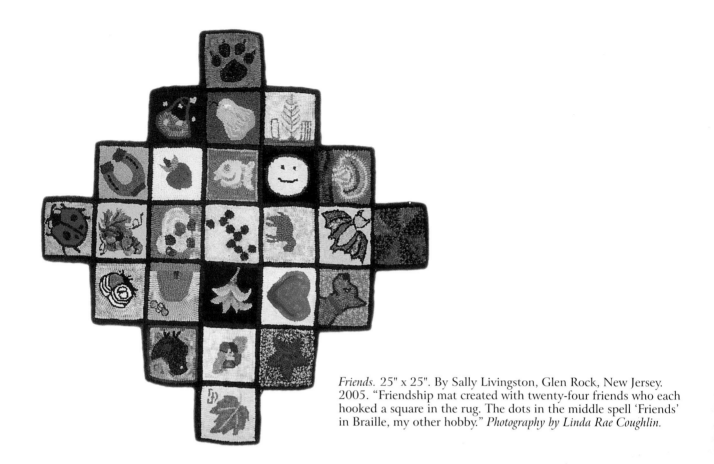

Friends. 25" x 25". By Sally Livingston, Glen Rock, New Jersey. 2005. "Friendship mat created with twenty-four friends who each hooked a square in the rug. The dots in the middle spell 'Friends' in Braille, my other hobby." *Photography by Linda Rae Coughlin.*

Friendship. 30" x 50". By Edyth Locke, Teaneck, New Jersey. 2005. Friendship mat created with twenty-four friends who each hooked a square in the rug. *Photography by Linda Rae Coughlin.*

Chapter Eight
LOCATIONS

When it comes to creating either a group project or theme-related series by a single artist, the places that we know and love seem to be popular subjects.

CITIES IN YARN
BY VICTOR EMIL PELL

Victor Pell is a self-taught artist who uses a punch needle to create his cityscape rugs. His rugs capture the essence of a city in rug format. When designing, Victor feels that nothing is too small to exclude from the rug. Using a bird's-eye view to display buildings, parks, streets, and sidewalks, he finds that all objects have a function and purpose. As he walks the cities that he will design, sometimes being mistaken for a construction worker or city employee, he often uses the tops of rubbish containers as easels. Although his pieces are aerial views, he designs them from the ground up. The streets go in first; then the buildings are created from their footprints skyward. The varied sizes and heights of the hooked loops, with their brick-like look, help to delineate the protrusions and setbacks of the buildings.

Victor's goal is to present the beauty of cities, along with a historical document of each city at a specific point in history. The aerial view helps to show some of the relationships that exist between the buildings and the space around them. *Photography courtesy of Victor Emil Pell.*

Washington, D.C. 65" x 97". By Victor Emil Pell, Royal Oak, Michigan. 1981. "The Capitol in the foreground overlooks the National Mall with its Smithsonian Institution Buildings, the Washington Monument, the Lincoln Memorial and across the Potomac River to the distant Robert E. Lee Mansion (nestled atop Arlington National Cemetery on the upper left)."

Detroit Rug. 26" x 126". By Victor Emil Pell, Royal Oak, Michigan. 1979. "My first historical cityscape hooked rug was designed soon after the construction of the Renaissance Center complex, which has become General Motors World Headquarters (located right of center). This rug shows Detroit's skyline as it appeared from Windsor, Ontario, Canada."

Toronto. 81" x 36". By Victor Emil Pell, Royal Oak, Michigan. 1984. "This piece captures the city of Toronto celebrating its 100th Anniversary, and at the same time the Province of Ontario celebrating its 150th Anniversary. Toronto's City Hall is the white circular complex in the foreground. The Parliament building is at the top, directly above the circular green grounds."

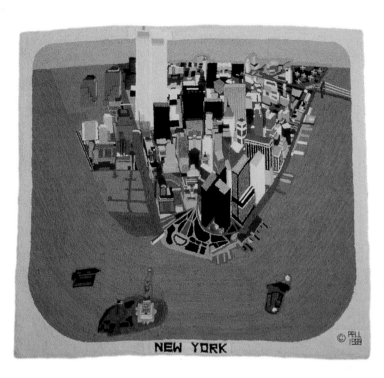

New York. 71" x 77". By Victor Emil Pell, Royal Oak, Michigan. 1986. "This is an aerial view of New York City harbor and lower Manhattan. It depicts New York as it appeared during the Statue of Liberty's Centennial Celebration in 1986. The Brooklyn Bridge is on the upper right. The two tall white buildings at the top were the World Trade Center towers. Since 9/11/2001, the meaning of the New York Rug has changed for me. The large amount of sand visible on the west side of lower Manhattan was dug out of the World Trade Center site and moved to expand the island. The sand became some of the foundation ground for Battery Park City. Now when I look at the rug, I think of the sand as holy ground, just like the original World Trade Center site. I am grateful to have captured this sand before the rest of Battery Park City was built on it."

Chicago. 77" x 60". By Victor Emil Pell, Royal Oak, Michigan. 1999. "This rug documents Chicago's appearance at the turn of the Millennium. In the piece, the Chicago River and Michigan Avenue intersect diagonally. It is fitting that Chicago's skyscrapers are depicted in this rug, as they originated in Chicago and rug hooking first started in North America."

PATHWAYS

This series was the result of a class taught by fiber artist Peg Irish. Peg wanted to promote spontaneity in her students, so she asked them to have only a basic idea of what they would create, with nothing preplanned–not even the color or design–before they came to her class. In class, they all decided on a unified theme for the series which they could interpret any way they chose. Shown here are some examples of what was created in that class.

Log Cabin Clearing. 22" x 27". By Peg Irish, Madberry, New Hampshire. 2005. *Courtesy of Peg Irish.*

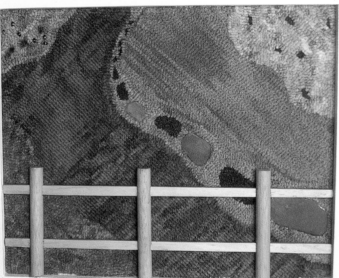

Abstract Garden. 9" x 12". By Sandra J. Barnhart, Barre, Vermont. 2005. Abstract garden, mixed media. *Photography by Linda Rae Coughlin.*

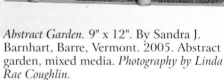

June Bride. 22" x 33". By Diane Proctor, Wilton, New Hampshire. 2004. "Pathways" bride and groom at a church in a village in New England. *Courtesy of Diane Proctor.*

April Showers. 17" x 23". By Arlene Jackman,
Vergennes, Vermont. 2004. Children, both born
in April, returning home from camp. *Courtesy of
Arlene Jackman.*

December. 14" x 18". By Peggy Stanilonis,
Vergennes, Vermont. 2005. "A winter wood-
land with animals and birds present in the
woods with a log cabin." *Courtesy of Peggy
Stanilonis.*

Beautiful Swimmer. 24" x 18". By Sally D'Albora,
Rockville, Maryland. 2004. "These swimmers are
on a path from their cozy dwelling at the bottom
of the Chesapeake to the cookpot." *Courtesy of Sally
D'Albora.*

LIVING ON CAPE COD

The theme for this series was created by a group of ten fiber artists who decided to document the landscape and sea of their beloved Cape Cod. All the pieces in this series measure about 15" x 18".

My Home. By Bette Barker, Orleans, Massachusetts. 2003. "My house was built in 1840, and in the original part of the house Josiah Crosby and his wife brought up their eight children." *Courtesy of Bette Barker.*

Mermaid. By Patsy Becker, South Orleans, Massachusetts. 2002. Mermaid in a boat with original flags denoting Cape Cod. *Courtesy of Patsy Becker.*

Lobster. By Barbara Bernard, East Orleans, Massachusetts. 2002. A red lobster with a checkerboard border. *Courtesy of Barbara Bernard.*

Eastham Windmill. By Sylvia Campbell, Eastham, Massachusetts. 2002. The windmill in Eastham, MA. *Courtesy of Sylvia Campbell.*

Smiling Red Crab. By Carolyn Creavy, East Orleans, Massachusetts. 2002. Red crab with scallop shells. *Courtesy of Carolyn Creavy.*

There Is No Place Like Home. By Bonnie de Blij, Chatham, Massachusetts. 2002. "The view from my back door overlooking Chatham Harbor." *Courtesy of Bonnie de Blij.*

Serenity. By Natalie DiPaolo, Brewster, Massachusetts. 2002. Ocean scene with a sailboat. *Courtesy of Natalie DiPaolo.*

Outermost House. By Susan McDonald, Eastham, Massachusetts. 2002. *Courtesy of Susan McDonald.*

My Cape Cod. By Marian Gray, South Orleans, Massachusetts. 2002. "This was the house we spent our summers in on Cape Cod, with its grassy and bearberry dunes and the bay nearby." *Courtesy of Marian Gray.*

Nauset Harbor From Snow's Bluff. By Jean E. Snow, Eastham, Massachusetts. 2002. "This rug depicts the view from our summer home at Snow's Bluff." *Courtesy of Jean E. Snow.*

RURAL AMERICA
BY MARY ANNE WISE

Of her landscape rugs, Mary Anne Wise writes:

My original motivation for hooking landscapes grew out of my frustration in trying to influence land use development issues in my rural community. Controlling my own worlds in hooked landscapes was a refreshing relief from endless committee meetings, as well as being rabidly badgered by the angry property rights fringe.

Rooted in the landscape of western Wisconsin's farm fields, woods, and waterways, I like to arrange images in tribute to long views and countryside I call home. It's good to be Queen in my very own landscapes, where I have the first and last word on what goes on and what happens where. *Photography courtesy of Mary Anne Wise.*

Domestic Heat. 34" x 40". By Mary Anne Wise, Stockholm, Wisconsin. 2003. *Private collection.*

Sanctuary. 29" x 46". By Mary Anne Wise, Stockholm, Wisconsin. 2005. *Private collection.*

Fading Flotsam. 39" x 61". By Mary Anne Wise, Stockholm, Wisconsin. 2005. *Private collection.*

Lilly Light. 24" x 39". By Mary Anne Wise, Stockholm, Wisconsin. 2005. *Private collection.*

THE CANADIAN LANDSCAPE

Working together as a group for the past few years, "Les Hookeuses du Bor'de'lo" of Shediac, New Brunswick, Canada has taken many different subjects and developed them into rugs. Featured here are some examples of rugs they created with a landscape theme. *Photography by Christian Ouellet.*

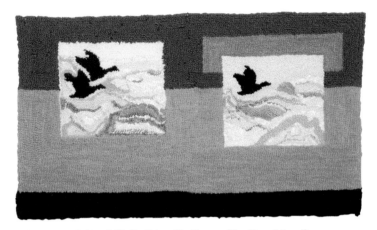

Transition. 24" x 36". By Line Godbout, Shediac, New Brunswick, Canada. 2005. "While walking, I saw two Canada geese flying in unison and could not help comparing my life with my companion of more than thirty years who recently passed away. I now continue my life without this exceptional man and know that my life has been enriched by his presence and that I am still blessed with golden sunsets."

Sailing Away. 28" x 24". By Thérèsa Arsenault Léger, Shediac, New Brunswick, Canada. 2005. "On my walks on the beach in the summer and fall, I gather old pieces of rope, faggots, and driftwood. These objects inspired this two-part piece of sailboats like the ones I see in the Bay of Cocagne near our cottage."

Seashells. 33" x 24". By Helena Bourque, Shediac, New Brunswick, Canada. 2005. "Walking on the beach, I look for seashells. As my worries disappear, I think of fond memories of my childhood playing on the beach."

My Sycamore. 30" x 28". By Jeanne Bourgeois, Grande-Digue, New Brunswick, Canada. 2003. This piece is the companion piece to a poem Jeanne wrote about a sycamore tree.

The Scarecrow. 32" x 25". By Linda Corbin, She-diac, New Brunswick, Canada. 2005. "In spring, the scarecrow is a protector. Come summer, he is a perch for the crows. In the fall, he waits for children looking for candy and surprises. In the winter, he is tired of all his hardships and is transformed into a windmill of torn clothes."

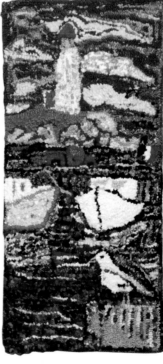

The Aboiteau Wharf. 27" x 55". By Annie Richard, Cape-Pelé, New Brunswick, Canada. 2005. "Walking on the wharf, I enjoy hearing all the fishermen's stories. This three-part piece captures the scenery, colors, and boats of my surroundings."

OTHER LOCATION RUGS

Some additional examples of rugs that were hooked to depict a specific location.

Buchanan Barn. 19" x 31". By Helen Buchanan, Ringoes, New Jersey. 2005. "Big red barn with American flag displayed after 9/11. Farm now owned by son Joe and his wife TC." *Photography by Linda Rae Coughlin.*

Spring Fever. 36" x 32". By Danielle Ouellet, Grande-Digue, New Brunswick, Canada. 1998. A springtime theme inspired by her artist son's drawing at age five.

Historic Canaan Street. 23" x 69". By Kristina Burnett, Canaan, New Hampshire. 2005. "This runner depicts Canaan St. in Canaan, New Hampshire, as it is today–a vital community that preserved its rich heritage of nineteenth century architecture. The runner includes the old church, meeting house, museum, old Methodist church (now a private residence), and our home, the Currier House." *Photography by Kristina Burnett.*

Buchanan Homestead. 20" x 32". By Helen Buchanan, Ringoes, New Jersey. 1995. Buchanan family home in 1994, nestled in among the large trees. *Photography by Linda Rae Coughlin.*

The Mill. 27" x 38". By Ingrid C. Cosmen, Glen Gardner, New Jersey. 2005. Designed by Ingrid's husband, Franklin G. Cosmen. A typical mill in Hunterdon County, NJ *Photography by Linda Rae Coughlin.*

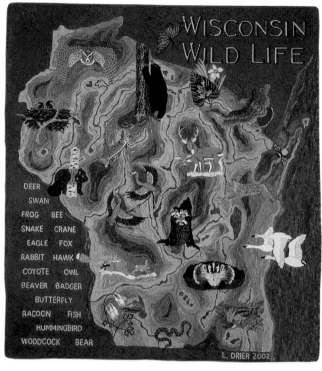

Wisconsin Wild Life. 66" x 60". By Lyle Drier, Waukesha, Wisconsin. 2002. The state of Wisconsin with some of the animals common to the area. *Photography by Larry Sanders.*

The Old Man. 24" round. By Peg Irish, Madberry, New Hampshire. 1989. "Designed for the League of New Hampshire Craftsmen's annual juried show. Subtitle 'The Muse of New Hampshire.' Won Ballentine 'Best in Show' Award." *Courtesy of Peg Irish.*

The Neighborhood. 36" x 36". By Tracy Jamar, New York City, New York. 2000. Nine houses, each one 12" square. A primitive house shape, hooked in brightly colored recycled t-shirts to make a flexible installation. Each house is mounted separately, to allow for a variety of arrangements. Shown here in a compact 3' x 3' grid. *Courtesy of Tracy Jamar.*

Treasures. 25" x 32". By Barbara Dalrymple Lugg, French-town, New Jersey. 2000. "For where your treasure is, there your heart may be also." *Photography by Linda Rae Coughlin.*

Peggy's Cove. 24" x 28". By Barbara Dalrymple Lugg, Frenchtown, New Jersey. 2001. Fishing shack at Peggy's Cove. *Photography by Linda Rae Coughlin.*

Wandering Landscape. 108" x 144". By Arne Nyen, Stock-holm, Wisconsin. 1994. Tufted rug. *Courtesy of Arne Nyen.*

Texas Ranch. 23" x 23". By Emily K. Robertson, Falmouth, Massachusetts. 2004. "This rug was made to act as a thank you gift from a large group of friends to our host and hostess, whose ranch is portrayed here. I didn't have high hopes for this rug because the composition wasn't as strong as I wished, but I used it to demonstrate differ-ent techniques while teaching a rug hooking class, and as sometimes happens this rug took off with a life of its own and turned out very well." *Photography by Diane Marshall.*

The Hudson River From Cold Spring. 30" x 43". By Alice Rudell, New York City, New York. 1995. This rug shows the wonderful view north from Cold Spring on the Hudson–the North Gate. *Courtesy of Alice Rudell.*

Bend in the River. 15" x 18". By Matilda K. Weeks, Port Murray, New Jersey. 2001. Designed by Joan Moshimer. *Photography by Linda Rae Coughlin.*

Historic Shelter Island. 32" x 38". By Elisabeth Williamson, Severna, Maryland. 2003. "Done to celebrate the 350th birthday of Shelter Island, the island where I grew up." *Courtesy of Elisabeth Williamson.*

Lighthouses. 42" round. By Elisabeth Williamson, Severna, Maryland. 2000. "These east coast lighthouses were chosen not only for their architectural diversity, but also the designer's special fondness for them." *Courtesy of Elisabeth Williamson.*

Sow Only the Good and Reap the Heavens. 28" x 36". By Ann Winterling, Concord, New Hampshire. 1992. A scene from the Shaker Village in Canterbury, NH. Bertha and Gertrude descending the path from the meeting house. Maple trees planted to celebrate all the orphans raised in the village, one for each child. A gift to Eldress Bertha. *Photography by Dwayne Bailey.*

Chapter Nine
SEASONS

Seasons can mean many things to many people, from the four seasons in the year, to the seasons of change in a person's life. Shown in this chapter are some of the many wonderful ways artists express change in their art.

THE SEASONS OF THE YEAR BY SUSAN FELLER

Susan Feller has hooked this series of five pieces to illustrate the changing of the seasons of the year. In this series, she explores a variety of fiber manipulation techniques, such as punch, traditional hooking, quilting, couching, beading, trapunto, needle felting, and bullet shell. She has also explored the use of many different materials, such as wool, linen thread, recycled sweaters, nylon, silk ribbons, crocheted lace, and more.

Susan writes about her series:

There are five seasons in this series, beginning with 'Spring.' Physically, our bodies adjust to the climate changes of the seasons. The diet should follow what is seasonally available, rather than a global satisfaction of our mental wants. In early summer, fresh new material is consumed and as late summer arrives the ingredients become heartier, preparing us for the fall and the long winter.

Although these pieces are my first attempt at mixed media and technique artwork, they are not the last. I felt energized and creative throughout this process. *Photography by Linda Rae Coughlin.*

Spring. 13" x 14". By Susan Feller, Augusta, West Virginia. 2005.

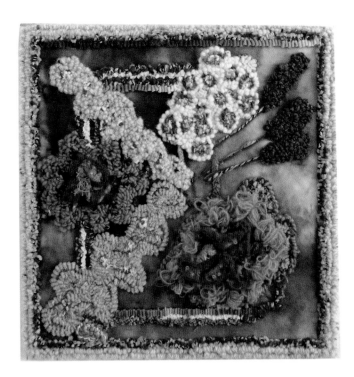

Early Summer. 14" x 15". By Susan Feller, Augusta, West Virginia. 2005.

Late Summer Harvest. 14" x 14". By Susan Feller, Augusta, West Virginia. 2005. Early August harvest with hayroll, pokeberry fruits, pumpkins, and gourds ripening.

Homestead Fall. 13" x 14". By Susan Feller, Augusta, West Virginia. 2005. A log cabin's warm inviting doorway, fall foliage, and grapes.

Winter. 13" x 14". By Susan Feller, Augusta, West Virginia. 2005.

THE CEDAR CHEST SERIES
BY MATILDA K. WEEKS

Upon receiving her grandfather's cedar chest, Matilda Weeks decided to use it as a coffee table. For protection of the wood, she decided to hook a rug cover, and hence the Cedar Chest series was conceived. The original idea was for four seasonal designs, which then became the twelve months of the year. To date, five of the pieces are completed with the others expected to be completed within the next few years. *Photography by Linda Rae Coughlin.*

Frosty Nights. 19" x 40". By Matilda K. Weeks, Port Murray, New Jersey. 2003. Cedar chest piece for the month of January. Designed by Black Bird Design – Adams & Allen.

Kodiak Showers. 19" x 40". By Matilda K. Weeks, Port Murray, New Jersey. 2003. Cedar chest piece for the month of April. Design from "Painted Ladies" by Barbara Landee. Matilda has two grandchildren who live in Kodiak, Alaska, and who love to dance with their umbrellas in the rain.

Stained Glass Flowers. 19" x 40". By
Matilda K. Weeks, Port Murray, New
Jersey. 2002. Cedar chest piece for
the month of August. Designed by
Sibbelly.

My Pumpkins Shine Too. 19" x 40".
By Matilda K. Weeks, Port Murray,
New Jersey. 2001. Cedar chest piece
for the month of October. Adapted
from Patti Patrick's "Pumpkin
Moonshine," *Rug Hooking Magazine,*
Volume XII #2 September/October
2000.

Angel in Flight. 19" x 40". By Matilda
K. Weeks, Port Murray, New Jersey.
2004. Cedar chest piece for the month
of December. Designed by Sherri
Hieber Day.

VIEW OVER ROWNTREE PARK
BY LOUISA CREED

"These four pieces are of my view over Rowntree Park, York, England. In Autumn of 1996, the view and light from my rooftop study was so spectacular that I decided to capture it in a rug. Later that year it snowed, which gave birth to the next rug in this four season series." *Photography and artist's statement courtesy of Louisa Creed.*

Autumn. 40" x 58". By Louisa Creed, York, England. 1996. First piece created in the series.

Winter. 40" x 58". By Louisa Creed, York, England. 1996.

Spring. 40" x 58". By Louisa Creed, York, England. 1996.

Creativity is not subject to cause or effect.

Summer. 40" x 58". By Louisa Creed, York, England. 1997.

FANTASY TREE SERIES

This "Fantasy Tree" series was designed by Stacy LeCure, a member of the Colonial Rug Hookers of Northern Virginia. The artists who participated in the project were able to interpret their tree design any way they chose. This collection shows some wonderful examples of creativity, fun, and imagination.

Untitled. 16" x 19". By Ann Campany, Vienna, Virginia. 2005. A bare tree with cardinals and a snowman. *Courtesy of Ann Campany.*

Fall. 20" x 19". By Rebecca Cridler, Charles Town, West Virginia. 2005. A fall tree with leaves. *Courtesy of Rebecca Cridler.*

Seasons. 16" x 20". By Dorothy Gorham, Lorton, Virginia. 2004. "The four seasons in one apple tree, with the spring blooms, summer leaves, fall apples, and colored leaves and winter with the bare branches covered in snow." *Courtesy of Dorothy Gorham.*

Tree Fantasy. 16" x 19". By Elizabeth Kaplowitz, Reston, Virginia. 2005. Tree silhouetted against evening sky. A dark border with the four phases of the moon in the corners. *Courtesy of Elizabeth Kaplowitz*

Sweet Autumn. 17" x 20". By Stacy R. LeCure, Bristow,
Virginia. 2004. *Courtesy of Stacy R. LeCure.*

Solitude. 36" x 24". By Andria Legon,
Annandale, Virginia. 2005. Inlaid in a
penny rug. *Courtesy of Andria Legon.*

Untitled. 15" x 18". By Barbara Personette, Fairfax, Virginia.
2005. Embellished with proddy, needle felting, and felt.
Courtesy of Barbara Personette.

Winter Wonder. 19" x 18". By Mary B. Tycz, Falls Church, Virginia.
2003. "A winter scene with a tree against a large moon. This rug
appeared in *Rug Hooking Magazine's* publication *A Celebration of
Hand-Hooked Rugs XIV.*" *Courtesy of Mary Tycz.*

SEASONS OF A WOMAN
BY EMILY ROBERTSON

Emily Robertson likes to push the envelope and explore subjects that are meaningful to her. She writes about this series:

A few years ago, a fellow rug hooker told me that I didn't have enough personality in my work. While this surprised me, it also gave me food for thought. I decided to do a series that showed aspects of all women's lives. One thing that all women have in common is menstruation, either in the past or present. I wanted to see whether there was any imagery using blood that could be still seen as benign and perhaps humorous. I decided to make a series of pieces exploring the responses I and my women friends have had to the menstrual process throughout our lives. I wanted to choose only positive responses to what is just a natural bodily fluid. In the first piece, entitled "Not Now," I used my friend's legs and Mary Jane shoes for my imagery. Working on these smaller pieces in between larger works, I have completed a series of eight. In "Joy" and "Sorrow," the final two pieces in the series, I used my friend's legs and feet again as I had in the first one. This time the imagery had a double meaning, as they also commemorate the death and loss of my friend and serve as a reminder of what she brought to my life.

Not shown but part of the series is, "Comfort." 2003. *Private collection.*

Not Now. 20" x 17". By Emily K. Robertson, Falmouth, Massachusetts. 2003. First piece in this series. "I used an image of Patty Yoder's feet and legs because she had such cute Mary Janes on that day and because I wanted to catch the way she was standing." *Private Collection. Photography by Linda Rae Coughlin.*

Prayers Answered. 20" x 17". By Emily K. Robertson, Falmouth, Massachusetts. 2003. "This piece has multiple messages about women's perceptions. It expresses the complexity of our lives." *Private Collection. Courtesy of Sharon L. Townsend.*

No Shame. 17" x 21". By Emily K. Robertson, Falmouth, Massachusetts. 2003. "I used a friend's clogs for this rug. I wanted to convey that women need never apologize for the way they are in life's adventure." *Photography by Diane Marshall.*

Patriotic Period. 21" x 23". By Emily K. Robertson, Falmouth, Massachusetts. 2004. "This rug is just what it appears to be, a patriotic period! I loved the fun I had putting it together with the somewhat Federalist lettering and the red, white, and blue motif. I knew it was special when I added the shoe laces." *Photography by Diane Marshall.*

Keep an idea journal. When you get an idea, write it down. Refer to it when you have one of those "dry" times without ideas.

No Way. 21" x 23". By Emily K. Robertson, Falmouth, Massachusetts. 2004. "I especially wanted to convey how a sophisticated woman might respond to the dilemma I had been portraying in the other rugs in this series. I used Susan Smidt's Illusion Wool to great advantage in these stylish shoes." *Photography by Diane Marshall.*

Joy. 25" x 25". By Emily K. Robertson, Falmouth, Massachusetts. 2005. "While I had always had these two images 'Joy' and 'Sorrow' in my mind as the conclusion to this menstruation series, it wasn't until Patty Yoder died in the Spring of 2005 that I realized that I had to use her legs, feet, and shoes as my concluding images. I wanted to do two pieces that were nearly identical but that would show how different the same experience can be from different attitudes. It is my memorial to Patty that she could bring us such joy and at the same time such concluding sorrow." *Photography by Diane Marshall.*

Sorrow. 24" x 26". By Emily K. Robertson, Falmouth, Massachusetts. 2005. The last piece in the series. *Photography by Diane Marshall.*

OTHER SEASONS OF THE YEAR RUGS

Featured here are some delightful rugs also having to do with the seasons in the year.

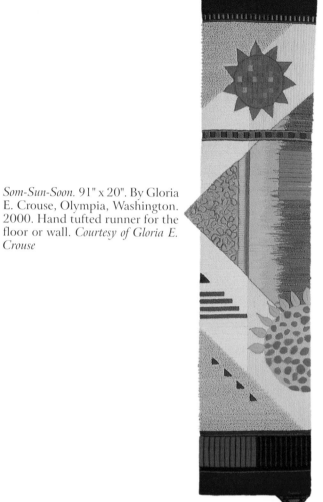

Som-Sun-Soon. 91" x 20". By Gloria E. Crouse, Olympia, Washington. 2000. Hand tufted runner for the floor or wall. *Courtesy of Gloria E. Crouse*

Winter Bloom. 18" x 11". By Tonya Benson, Marietta, Ohio. 2005. *Courtesy of Tonya Benson.*

Yule Roses. 18" x 23". By Ingrid C. Cosmen, Glen Gardner, New Jersey. 2001. Yule roses are the Swedish name for poinsettias. Designed by Ingrid's husband Franklin G. Cosmen with loving memories of Ingrid's grandmother, who filled the house with poinsettias at Christmas time. *Photography by Linda Rae Coughlin.*

Spring. 39" x 55". By Patti Ann Finch, Medford, New Jersey. 2004. *Courtesy of Patti Ann Finch.*

Flower Power. 38" x 51". By Patti Ann Finch, Medford, New Jersey. 2004. *Courtesy of Patti Ann Finch.*

Finch Family Fun. 41" x 54". By Patti Ann Finch, Medford, New Jersey. 2002. *Courtesy of Patti Ann Finch.*

Snow People. 36" x 28". By Joyce Krueger, Waukesha, Wisconsin. 1998. "There are many ways to dress a snowman, but not enough time to make a rug of each." *Courtesy of Joyce Krueger.*

Welcome To My Garden. 21" x 28". By Barbara Dalrymple Lugg, Frenchtown, New Jersey. 1999. Toads and spiders in the garden with the black-eyed Susans. *Photography by Linda Rae Coughlin.*

Glory. 39" x 25". By Diane S. Learmonth, Anacortes, Washington. 2004. "One day I was raking up oak leaves in our yard and this rug came to me. The leaves on the rug are the actual size and shape of the ones in my yard. Autumn is my favorite time of year and I think it must be God's too, because he does such a beautiful job with it." *Courtesy of Diane Learmonth.*

Basket and Apple Bucket. 22" x 31". By Karen Maddox, Kerrville, Texas. 2004. "This is the first piece I hooked with words in the border." *Courtesy of Karen Maddox.*

Winter Guest. 24" x 28". By Barbara Dalrymple Lugg, Frenchtown, New Jersey. 2002. *Photography by Linda Rae Coughlin.*

Lady Slipper With Spring Peeper. 17" x 15". By Julie Robinson, Loudon, New Hampshire. 2005. "I am originally from Minnesota and remember getting such excitement out of finding Minnesota's state flowers, the showy lady slippers!" *Courtesy of Julie Robinson.*

Camp at Cherry Mountain. 20" x 24". By Julie Robinson, Loudon, New Hampshire. 2004. "My husband and I have a camp in the White Mountains of New Hampshire. This rug was designed from one of the many memories we have from our visits there." *Courtesy of Julie Robinson.*

Sweet Sugar Afternoon. 21" x 29". By Julie Robinson, Loudon, New Hampshire. 2005. "In early spring we help a good friend make maple syrup at his sugarhouse. Often when we step outside there are deer around the sugarhouse." *Courtesy of Julie Robinson.*

OTHER SEASONS OF LIFE RUGS

Some are wonderful rugs that have to do with "seasons" in a person's life.

Evolution of a Woman. 10" x 48". By Linda Rae Coughlin, Warren, New Jersey. 2004. "A study of the evolution of a woman from birth, to adolescence, to full womanhood, to old age, and finally to death." *Photography by Linda Rae Coughlin.*

The Dare. 27" x 25". By Burma Cassidy, Rochester, Vermont. 2005. "The moment of overcoming fear and courageously jumping!" *Courtesy of Burma Cassidy.*

Woman in Room. 20" round. By Sarah Nickerson, Stockton Spring, Maine. 2000. Private Collection. *Photography by Linda Rae Coughlin.*

3:00 A.M. 18" x 24". By Diane S. Learmonth, Anacortes,
Washington. 2005. "Most of the women I know, including myself, are awake around 3:00 A.M. I just lie there,
but many women are very productive during this time of
night." *Courtesy of Diane Learmonth.*

Playing at Control and Losing… 30" x 40". By Diane S. Learmonth,
Anacortes, Washington. 2005. "I designed this rug in a rage.
Three women were trying to box me in with my creativity and I
decided to have nothing to do with it. This is a self portrait and as
you can see they lost the battle." *Courtesy of Diane Learmonth.*

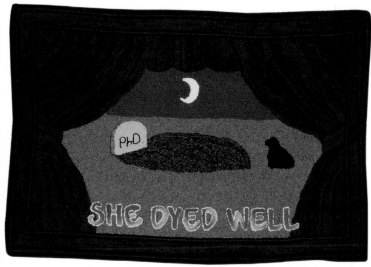

She Dyed Well. 26" x 40". By Emily K. Robertson, Falmouth,
Massachusetts. 2001. "This is my epitaph rug and, I feel,
sums up the quality and accomplishments of my life. The
concept for it came out of a conversation I had with a friend
and I drew and hooked it very quickly. When I was com-
pleting my doctoral work, many people would ask me what
I was going to do with my degree. I would flippantly reply
that it would look good on a tombstone, which it certainly
does in this scene. My dear dog, Betsy, sits as a mourner at
the foot of the grave and the rainbow writing 'she dyed well'
reflects the joy I have had in rug hooking." *Photography by
Diane Marshall.*

Chapter Ten
SIGNS, DOOR TOPPERS, AND MATS

Working on a small mat or doing a study piece of a single design element can be a very good opportunity for trying something new. Featured here are some fun and creative signs, mats, and door toppers.

DOOR TOPPERS
BY THE ALICE BEATTY GUILD

A few years ago, the Alice Beatty Chapter of ATHA of North Plainfield, New Jersey, decided to create a door topper challenge for its guild members. Featured here are eight rugs from that challenge.
Photography by Linda Rae Coughlin.

Flying Angel. 9" x 29". By Margaret Lutz, Flemington, New Jersey. 1997.

Santa. 11" x 22". By Sharon Ballard, Lebanon, New Jersey. 1997.

From This Day Forward. 11" x 30". By Linda Rae Coughlin, Warren, New Jersey. 1997. "A piece to mark our wedding day."

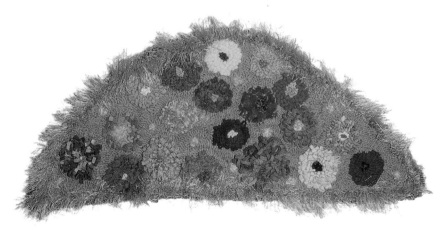

A Thirst For Color. 18" x 28". By Matilda K. Weeks, Port Murray, New Jersey. 2005.

146

Village. 14" x 20". By Barbara Dalrymple Lugg, Frenchtown, New Jersey. 2005.

Pika & Cody. 17" x 44". By Claudia Casebolt, Lawrenceville, New Jersey. 1997.

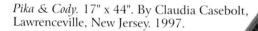

I Ain't Going... 11" x 28". By Janet Bosshard, Lebanon, New Jersey. 2005.

Love, Peace, Joy. 8" x 37". By Janet Santaniello, Watchung, New Jersey. 2000.

BORDER SERIES
BY JUDY QUINTMAN

Judy Quintman, of Wilmington, North Carolina, decided to do a study in borders to see how they change the look of a rug.
Photography courtesy of Judy Quintman.

Ed. 28" x 26". By Judy Quintman, Wilmington, North Carolina. 2001. "This was the first rug in the border series and one of my first original designs."

Barney. 23" x 30". By Judy Quintman, Wilmington, North Carolina. 2001. Border series.

Bouquet. 29" x 38". By Judy Quintman, Wilmington, North Carolina. 2004. "This series started with animals and has branched out to other things."

Art is lived in the spirit of play.

Cat. 18" x 30". By Judy Quintman, Wilmington, North Carolina. 2004. Heart border series. "This series has three pieces for now but many more to come."

Sheep. 19" x 30". By Judy Quintman, Wilmington, North Carolina. 2002. Heart border series.

Birds. 20" x 30". By Judy Quintman, Wilmington, North Carolina. 2003. Heart border series.

OTHER SIGNS,
DOOR TOPPERS, AND MATS

Enjoy the Passage. 10" x 23". By Burma Cassidy, Rochester, Vermont. 2006. A reminder to take time. *Courtesy of Burma Cassidy.*

Welcome. 26" x 48". By Karen Maddox, Kerrville, Texas. 1999. "This was hooked with coat weight wool my mother had saved for thirty years." *Courtesy of Karen Maddox.*

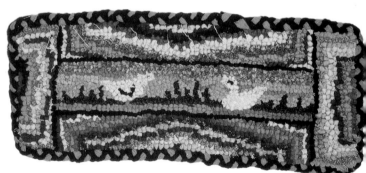

Two Ducks. 10" x 22". By Sarah Nickerson, Stockton Spring, Maine. 2000. *Private Collection. Photography by Linda Rae Coughlin.*

Croatian Croni. 12" x 54". By Carole K. Bartolovic, Avon, Ohio. 2004. "'Old Crow Inn announces the proprietorship of our home on the north coast of Ohio." *Courtesy of Carole Bartolovich.*

PA Bird. 13" x 18". By Tonya Benson, Marietta,
Ohio. 2005. *Courtesy of Tonya Benson.*

Cigar Store Punch. 48" x 31". By Lyle
Drier, Waukesha, Wisconsin. 2004.
"The central motif is an antique cigar
store figure that my husband and I
own." *Courtesy of Lyle Drier.*

Denise's Pumpkin. 24" x 16". By Margaret Lutz,
Flemington, New Jersey. 1994. "Made for my
granddaughter, Denise. Piece is mounted on a
wooden board and is free standing." *Photography
by Linda Rae Coughlin.*

Chapter Eleven
OF UNIVERSAL APPEAL

Included in this chapter are some fascinating rugs that have universal appeal because of their interesting subject matter and global content.

A BOY FROM ORIENT BY GAIL F. HORTON

Gail Horton created this series after hearing many stories told by her husband, Dave Horton, about his growing up years in Orient, New York. Told with richness and a great sense of place, Dave's tales over the years translated from many times told oral tales to visual images for her. In addition to making occasional excursions to the sites in the stories, Gail started to tape her husband's tales of bye-gone days in Orient, and hooked tapestries emerged from these stories.

Being very involved with the Oysterponds Historical Society, this project was supported in part with funds from the Special Opportunity Stipend (S.O.S.) program through the New York Foundation for the Arts, administered on Long Island by the East End Arts Council. *Photography courtesy of Gail F. Horton.*

Rum War on the Sound: March 30, 1932. 20" x 19". By Gail F. Horton, Greenport, New York. 2004. "On March 30, 1932, Prohibition was still in force. My very pregnant mother–I was due in two days–and her mother were returning from the movies in Greenport in my grandmother's 1920s Chrysler coupe with yellow, wooden-spoke wheels. As they were crossing the beaches in Orient they heard bingety-bang-boom out on the sound and they saw flashing lights and what looked like explosions. They got out of the car and watched the Coast Guard chasing down a rumrunner. My mother got so excited, she went into labor and her mother turned the car around and took her back to Greenport Hospital. I was born at 7:20 the next morning. I have always thanked the Coast Guard for saving me from being born on April Fool's Day."

The 1938 Hurricane. 19" x 23". By Gail F. Horton, Greenport, New York. 2004. "When the mercury popped out of the barometer in my first grade classroom, our teacher knew that the day's stormy weather was really serious. She told the principal and they called the parents to come take us home. Mom picked me and four other kids up and started on the half-mile journey home from the Orient Union Grammar School. As we drove down Tabor Road, next to the cemetery, a huge maple tree fell down in front of our 1920s Chrysler Coupe. While Mom was turning around to head the other way, another maple fell to the rear of the car, blocking her in. A farmer came along and rescued us, and took us to his home. After several more misadventures, we finally reached home about seven hours later. That hurricane of September 21, 1938 changed the landscape of Long Island forever wherever the mighty storm struck."

Orient School. 27" x 26". By Gail F. Horton, Greenport, New York. 2003. "I started first grade at the age of five in the Orient Union Grammar School. The school has been moved and is now the studio of sculptor Bob Berks. The school had first through eighth grades, and each classroom had two grades. When my class graduated and went to Greenport School, there were two of us in the class. When I was in seventh grade, my mother told me that my great-great-grandfather and my great-grandfather, Ezra and James Henry Young, built the school. I was very proud."

Sounds of Orient - Sunday Morning. 38" x 14". By Gail F. Horton, Greenport, New York. 2004. "My ears tell me more than my eyes. I would lie in bed at night and could hear the Cornfield Lightship and the bell buoy out near bug light. I could hear the train going over the bridge in Essex, Connecticut and I could recognize the sound of almost everyone's car in Orient. I loved to hear the different dogs bark and call out to one another. On Sunday morning, the bells of the Methodist Church that was across the park from our house rang and my dog, Bob, who had a wonderful voice, would sing to these bells. He would sit out on the sidewalk next to our kitchen door, with the wisteria arbor in the background and put his head up and howl." *From the collection of Pamela Vogt and Angela Andetta.*

Family Portrait – Five Generations. 21" x 24". By Gail F. Horton, Greenport, New York. 2005. "One time my mother said to me 'there's an elderly lady who's bedridden and probably won't last a year and she wants to see you because she saw Ezra Young, and James Henry Young. She's known our family a long time and she wants to see if you have the Young's family resemblance and to say she's seen five generations of one family before she dies.' So Mom took me down to her house and the old lady was stuck in her bed and she was very, very happy to see me, and she looked me over and said, 'Yes, you certainly do have the family resemblance.'"

Sunday Night Bath. 21" x 19". By Gail F. Horton, Greenport, New York. 2006. "My younger brother, Stewie, and I were young boys and we dreaded our weekly Sunday night bath. Mom enticed us to the tub by playing the radio during our weekly session. With ferocious lectures about electrocution from Mom that kept us terrified of touching the radio, we happily soaked away in the Linit-filled bath listening to the likes of Jack Benny, Fred Allen, Charlie McCarthy, Edgar Bergen, and Mortimer Snerd. We had toys and stuff to play with, and if Mom wasn't looking we would get a good tidal wave sloshing. Mom, much to our displeasure, vigorously scrubbed us down with a bristle brush and finished the bath off with a Halo shampoo and a rinse with lemon juice. We were certainly squeaky clean in the end."

Orient Potato Dock. 12" x 35". By Gail F. Horton, Greenport, New York. 2004. "The I.M. Young potato grading house was located on the dock on the end of my street, Village Lane. Flatbed trucks loaded with sacks of potatoes picked by hand from the local farm fields would come to unload the crop to be graded and put into the appropriate bags. Then the bags of potatoes would be loaded on trailer trucks or on local boats to be shipped to markets. When nobody was looking and the boat was empty, we kids would dive off the roof of the wheelhouse of the potato boat and bring up a potato, which showed up very nicely in the muddy bottom, to prove that we had made it all the way to the bottom." *From the collection of Jon Turner and Margaret Helfand.*

An Orient Evening. 20" x 25". By Gail F. Horton, Greenport, New York. 2005. "It was common back when I was a kid to have musical evenings in different people's homes. I remember one at Walter and Evelyn Kluge's house. Quite a collection of Orient people were there down at the point. Ruth Tabor and Helen Frost were very fine singers, Lloyd Terry played a one string viol, his wife, Martha, did monologues which were hilarious, and my parents would sing and play the piano. A couple of us kids also played whatever we had been taught recently. I remember this one evening because Evelyn Kluge was such a horrendously wonderful cook and she served elderberry upside-down cake–was it ever good." *From the collection of Priscilla Bull.*

Downtown Orient. 44" x 23". By Gail F. Horton, Greenport, New York. 2005. "My family home, built by my great-grandfather James Henry Young, was on Village Lane, the street that the three hundred inhabitants of the town called Downtown. There by the Mechanics Hall the kids used the telephone pole as a goal in wide-ranging games of kick the can. My brother Stew harnessed his dog to a sled to pull him through the snow in Hallelujah Park and farmers and duck hunters gathered at the Idle Hour during the day to pick up their mail and discuss local affairs."

Slave Cemetery Hog Pond, Orient. 28" x 20". By Gail F. Horton, Greenport, New York. 2005. "When I was a kid, Eliot Brooks, a pound fisherman and amateur archeologist, used to take me searching for arrowheads in the Hog Pond area where he tarred his nets. Once we came upon the Tuthill Family cemetery, where the family had buried with them some Poquatuck Indians and escaped slaves that came to their home, a station on the Underground Railroad. I was upset that the cemetery was in such disrepair and Eliot helped me to find someone with a scythe. After learning how to sharpen the tool, I borrowed it and cleaned up the cemetery so the gravestones showed."

Narrow River/Hallock's Bay. 18" x 59". By Gail F. Horton, Greenport, New York. 2003. "This site, where the arrow maker of the Poquatuck Indians once plied his trade, is a life-long favorite of mine. I used to go on sprightly walks with Eliot Brooks, who told me of his finds of Indian artifacts in the area and who swore that there were probably a dug out canoe or two buried in the silt of Narrow River. Friends and I used to trap muskrats there to sell the skins for spending money, and my brother and I still go clamming and scalloping out in Hallock's Bay. After the Poquatucks died off, the Hallock's Farm barrel house and wharf were located on this site. The only remnants of this self-sustaining enterprise are a few pilings out in the bay and pieces of concrete reinforced with old farm equipment that formed the floor of the barrel house, littered about the beach."

The End – Latham's Farm Orient, Long Island, New York. 18" x 66". By Gail F. Horton, Greenport, New York. 2003. "The Latham Farm, on the very end of the North Fork, on Orient Point was a family farm that was established in the eighteenth century and was farmed into the 1970s. This vibrant truck farm and small orchard, bounded by Gardiner's Bay, Plum Gut, and Long Island Sound, produced corn, string beans, cauliflower, lima beans, cabbage, and apples during the growing season. I used to harvest mussels on the flats at Orient Point leading out towards the rocks and the lighthouse when the waters of Plum Gut briefly exposed them at low tide. The End is a fall scene that includes the New London Ferry, *The Plum Island*, traversing the waters of Plum Gut with the Plum Island Lighthouse and water tower in the background on the left. The center of the triptych features the Latham Farm, the Orient Point Lighthouse, and one of the Latham's tying cauliflower prior to harvest. Orient Point Lighthouse, a lobster boat in Gardiner's Bay and more cauliflower form the right side." *From the collection of Peter and Mary Stevens.*

Skipper Horton Circa 1900. 15" x 17". By Gail F. Horton, Greenport, New York. 2003. "My dad had polio at the age of two, and went through life with a severe limp that prevented him from playing sports. Living surrounded by the sea in Greenport, he was fascinated by the water and at a young age rigged up the family sharpie with sails made of sheets using a couple of oars as a mast and boom. Steering with another oar, he sailed around the harbor using favorable tides and winds. His father helped him buy a Crosby Cat and in the summertime, when he reached his teens, he took sailing parties over to Shelter Island to hunt for birds' eggs. He got the nickname Skipper because of this."

North Fork Quartet – The Beaches. 77" x 44". By Gail F. Horton, Greenport, New York. 1999. "I have traveled the roads of Long Island all my life and nothing I have seen has changed my belief that the East Marion-Orient Causeway is the most beautiful stretch of road on this one hundred mile long island. The magnificent vistas, intriguing points of land, numerous bodies of water with all the attendant flora, bird life and maritime objects; this road leading to the sleepy harbor village of Orient shown in the distance speaks of the richness and beauty of small town life. When we were teenagers, we Orient kids always said that we wanted to cut Orient off at the beaches and have Mr. Greenhall's tug tow it down to Bermuda." *From the collection of Joshua Y. Horton.*

COMING HOME SERIES

"Coming Home" was a rug and literary exhibit exploring the perceptions of "Home" and held in 2005 at the Punderson Manor and Conference Center in Newbury, Ohio. It was sponsored by Cross Creek Farm Rug School and Habitat for Humanity of Geauga County, Ohio. Included here are samples of hooked pieces from that exhibit.

White Christmas in Greenport. 20" x 22". By Sarah J. McNamara, Greenport, New York. 2004. Because Sarah lives in a rather temperate area, snow is never guaranteed at Christmas. This rug was a gift to her husband Peter and daughter Clara. The border background is a black watch plaid given to Sarah's mother by her father more than four decades ago. This piece is one of her favorite rugs, with many memories hooked into it. She is happy that she doesn't have to shovel the snow from the sidewalk!. *Courtesy of Sarah J. McNamara.*

Habitat for Humanity: House and Home. 24" x 16". By Sarah J. McNamara, Greenport, New York. 2004. "The title for this piece comes from the idea that Habitat for Humanity not only builds houses, but builds homes for people. This rug resembles the house I grew up in, which has been home to four generations of our family. The doors stand open in invitation and the banner proudly proclaims 'Welcome Home' to its new inhabitants. This rug was donated to Habitat for Humanity of Geauga County, Ohio." *Courtesy of Sarah J. McNamara.*

Bucks' Leap. 15" x 60". By Fritz Mitnick, Pittsburgh, Pennsylvania. 2001. "Buildings on our farm at Bucks' Leap Indiana Township, PA. This rug received the President's Award." *Courtesy of Fritz Mitnick.*

Century Farm. 35" x 50". By Nancy J. Evans, Aurora, Ohio. 2004. Rug depicts family home. *Courtesy of Nancy J. Evans.*

Crab Apple Trees. 18" x 22". By Mary Logue, Golden Valley, Minnesota. 2004. "An impressionistic piece of my house in Stockholm, WI, when the apple blossoms are in bloom. Adapted from a photograph taken by Gerd Kreij." *Courtesy of Mary Logue.*

Our House. 25" x 35". By Nancy Karp, Chautauqua, New York. 2002. "I am a 'birder,' thus the birds in the border. We have six grandchildren, thus the eight cyclists in the border. Designed from a photograph taken by my husband, Norman." *Courtesy of Nancy Karp.*

Quilt Show. 30" x 40". By Susan Feller, Augusta, West Virginia. 2005. "This rug depicts things I think are important and memories of 'Home': a log cabin, me hanging quilts that depict America, our patriotism, and thriftiness. The bright colors evoke a cheerful and bright day." *Courtesy of Susan Feller.*

Welcome the unknown into your art.

The Way We Are. 16" x 20". By Susanne McNally, Curtisville, Pennsylvania. 1998. "The 'Retirement Rug.' Kids are gone, dad is pursuing his astronomy, and mom is walking the dog." *Courtesy of Susanne McNally.*

Indian Hunter. 25" x 36". By Cecilia Evans Clement, Manhattan, Kansas. 2005. An Índian hunting moose and deer from his canoe near a tepee.

CANADIAN RUGS
BY CECILIA E. CLEMENT

Cecilia Clement has taken the time to preserve history by reproducing (with permission) some of the antique Canadian rugs of the families of some of her local neighbors, from a part of Canada where she has summered since she was a child. All the rugs in this series were hooked with hand-cut strips of wool. *Photography courtesy of Cecilia Evans Clement.*

Three Grouse. 27" x 38". By Cecilia Evans Clement, Manhattan, Kansas. 2005. Grouse perched on a fallen tree over waterfalls.

Blue Moose. 26" x 37". By Cecilia Evans Clement, Manhattan, Kansas. 2004. Colorful moose, with blue bodies and red antlers. Interesting modern-looking hills and trees in the background.

Flying Geese. 26" x 40". By Cecilia Evans Clement, Manhattan, Kansas. 2002. Canadian geese with water lilies and cattails.

Bear in Old Tree. 13" x 23". By Cecilia Evans Clement, Manhattan, Kansas. 2004. Pillow of black bear with red maple leaves in corners.

Requiem for a Landscape. 30" x 15". By Karin L. Allen, Liverpool, Nova Scotia, Canada. 2004.

ART HITS THE WALL

"Art Hits The Wall" was a juried exhibition of unique quilted and hooked art created by residents of Atlantic Canada, which includes New Brunswick, Nova Scotia, Prince Edward Island, and Newfoundland. In 2004, this exhibit, curated by Trudi Curley, was held at the Rossignol Cultural Centre in Liverpool, Nova Scotia. The works showcased here are the thirty rugs from that exhibit. The goal of this show was for the artists in the exhibit to interpret the work of a "master" artist and then make a piece of their own in response to the original artwork. *Photography courtesy of Doris Eaton.*

The Happy Hooker. 32" x 40". By Jean Archer, Dartmouth, Nova Scotia, Canada. 2004.

The Creation of Eve or God and Eve. 18" x 24". By Myra Barss, LaHave, Nova Scotia, Canada. 2004.

Don't Step on Me. 40" x 32". By Valentine S. Bachmann, Bridgewater, Nova Scotia, Canada. 2004.

Lady of Leisure. 17" x 12". By Shirley I. Bradshaw, Yarmouth, Nova Scotia, Canada. 2004.

Red Cedar Memories. 36" x 20". By Mary Brown, Mill Village, Nova Scotia, Canada. 2004.

My Window. 22" x 15". By Marilyn Burns, Yarmouth, Nova Scotia, Canada. 2004.

Water Nymph. 21" x 26". By Celia Charlton, Hammonds Plains, Nova Scotia, Canada. 2004.

Madam Monet Hooking a Rug. 28" x 23". By Doris Eaton, Italy Cross, Nova Scotia, Canada. 2004.

Ships in a Storm. 27" x 39". By Chris Everill, West LaHave, Nova Scotia, Canada. 2004.

Under the Covers of Night. 41 inches in diameter. By Deanne Fitzpatrick, Amherst, Nova Scotia, Canada. 2004.

Harvest at La Crau. 19" x 23". By Margaret Geldart, Truro, Nova Scotia, Canada. 2004.

Tiger Man. 15" x 15". By Diane L. Harris, Gabarus, Nova Scotia, Canada. 2004.

Resettlement in Newfoundland. 25" x 20". By Diane Hodder, Charlottetown, Prince Edward Island, Canada. 2004.

In the Garden. 18" x 20". By Rita Jenkins, Shelburne, Nova Scotia, Canada. 2004.

The Road – Winter. 26" x 34". By Donna T. Johnson, Malagash, Nova Scotia, Canada. 2004.

D.A.M. 21" x 35". By Sarah Ladd, Pugwash Junction, Nova Scotia, Canada. 2004.

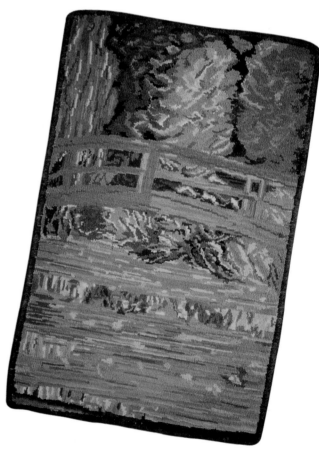

Green Harmony. 60" x 45". By Genevieve Laloux, Fredericton, New Brunswick, Canada. 2004.

Two Girls Reading. 18" x 12". By Edie Leger-Cole, Amherst, Nova Scotia, Canada. 2004.

Crazy Cubes. 36" x 36". By Fran Lewis, LaHave, Nova Scotia, Canada. 2004.

Memory of the Garden at Etten. 22" x 27". By Penny Lighthall, Truro, Nova Scotia, Canada. 2004.

My Angels. 23" x 35". By Diane MacDonald, Dartmouth, Nova Scotia, Canada. 2004.

The Haywain. 19" x 29". By Sylvia M. Macdonald, Pictou, Nova Scotia, Canada. 2004.

Not Another Driveway. 16" x 20". By Mollie "Lee" McBride, Waterville, Nova Scotia, Canada. 2004.

Another View of the Artist's Garden at Gilverny. 23" x 18". By Wendy Richardson, Bridgewater, Nova Scotia, Canada. 2004.

Home From the Woods. 15" x 17". By Jan Moir, Mill Village, Nova Scotia, Canada. 2004.

A Maritime Nativity. 31" x 35". By Nina Seaman, LaHave,
Nova Scotia, Canada. 2004.

Gulliver's Hole. 27" x 36". By Ruth Mills Smith, Springhill,
Nova Scotia, Canada. 2004.

Before the Storm, Blue Rocks, NS. 30" x 25". By Gwen Wilkie,
Pleasantville, Nova Scotia, Canada. 2004.

Bird Garden. 14" x 21". By Edith Wolter, Bridgewater,
Nova Scotia, Canada. 2004.

HISTORIC SITES
BY THE POTOMAC THRUMMERS

In early 2004, the Potomac Thrummers Rug Hooking Guild discussed working on a series of hooked rugs that would depict a historical event in the Washington, DC, Maryland, or Virginia area. The members of the guild who lived in one of these three areas chose a historical event of interest from their area to create a rug.

The Sandy Springs Museum, in historic Sandy Springs, Maryland, was enthusiastic about the project and expressed a desire to display the rugs. The rugs were displayed at the museum in the summer of 2004, along with original birdhouses that were built by local artists and based on historic buildings from the area.

Shown here are nine of the historical pieces that were created by some of the members of the Potomac Thrummers Rug Hooking Guild.

Marshall Hall. 12" x 17". By Barbara Barton, Bowie, Maryland. 2005. "Going to Marshall Hall Park on the River Queen, in Maryland for a fun day. Opened in 1889, closed in 1981." *Courtesy of Barbara Barton.*

National Zoo. 12" x 17". By Barbara Barton, Bowie, Maryland. 2005. "The front gates of the National Zoo in Washington, DC with all kinds of animals. It opened in 1886 with 163 acres and is part of the Smithsonian Institution." *Courtesy of Barbara Barton.*

O, Say Can You See? 12" x 17". By Barbara Barton, Bowie, Maryland. 2005. "Fort McHenry in Baltimore, Maryland was the site of the famous battle in 1814 that inspired Francis Scott Key to write the U.S. National Anthem, 'The Star Spangled Banner.'" *Courtesy of Barbara Barton.*

Thomas Point Lighthouse. 12" x 18". By Madeline Cholwek, Ashton, Maryland. 2005. "Thomas Point is the finest example of a Screw Pile Cottage anywhere in the world. It was manned until 1986. Located at the mouth of the South River, near Annapolis." *Courtesy of Madeline Cholwek.*

Carousel Horse. 13" x 18". By Judy Gardner, Burtonsville, Maryland. 2004. "The historic Dentzel Carousel at Glen Echo Park in Maryland was the inspiration for this piece. The horse is representative of one of the carousel's fifty-two wooden animals. Manufactured by the Philadelphia-based Dentzel Carousel Company, the carousel was installed at Glen Echo in 1921." *Courtesy of Judy Gardner.*

Sandy Spring Meeting House. 12" x 18". By Mary J. Noonan, Brookeville, Maryland. 2004. "Built in 1817, this was the third meeting house built since 1753 when the first Quakers/ Friends settled in the area." *Courtesy of Mary Noonan.*

Maryland's Liberty Tree. 12" x 18". By Barbara Rhoads, Derwood, Maryland. 2004. "Many of the thirteen colonies had Liberty Trees where colonists gathered to discuss independence politics. This one was located in Annapolis, Maryland on the grounds of St. John's College. It survived until 1999, when Hurricane Floyd destroyed it and it was cut down. It was the last surviving Liberty Tree and had witnessed the signing of the 1652 peace treaty between the Annapolis colonists and the Susquahannock Indians, a reception for Lafayette on his tour of Maryland in 1824, and numerous commencement exercises at the college." *Courtesy of Barbara Rhoads.*

Quilts of the Underground Railroad. 12" x 18". By Janet Sandberg, Silver Spring, Maryland. 2004. "Slave cabin with quilt hanging outside; border with single motif of quilt patterns purportedly used to guide escaped slaves via the underground railroad." *Courtesy of Janet Sandberg.*

Mount Vernon. 12" x 18". By Marie "Allene" Thibeault, Provincetown, Massachusetts. 2004. "Based on photograph taken in 1953 of me, at age five, with my mother and grandparents at Mt. Vernon on the lawn in front of George Washington's home." *Courtesy of Marie "Allene" Thibeault.*

OTHER GLOBAL STATEMENT RUGS

Included here are some other wonderful examples of rugs that make a global statement.

Women of the Congo. 52" x 26". By Donna K. Hrkman, Dayton, Ohio. 2005. "This piece was created for an organization called 'Woman for Woman International.' It draws attention to the genocide that has taken place and continues to happen in the Democratic Republic of the Congo, Sudan, Rwanda, South Africa, and elsewhere in Africa and Europe. This piece is both beautiful and horrific. It shows the desperation of a people to survive. What I hope to achieve in this piece is to motivate others. It is a tribute to the strength and dignity of the women, as well as a reminder that this type of cruelty must stop. We all don't have to sit idly by and watch. We can help. One person can make a difference. Words on the top of the rug read, 'Even a whisper can be heard above an army if it speaks the truth', words on the bottom, 'Decry the genocide taking place in Africa.'" *Courtesy of Donna Hrkman.*